THE MOJAVE

THE SAN BERNARDINOS

SAN GABRIEL VALLEY

THE SANTA ANAS

THE LOS ANGELES PLAIN

Los Angeles

A Sunset Pictorial

Los Angeles

Portrait of an extraordinary city

BY THE EDITORS OF SUNSET BOOKS AND SUNSET MAGAZINE

Supervising Editor: Paul C. Johnson, Editor of *Sunset* Books
Southwest Editor of *Sunset* Magazine: Walter Houk
Graphics Coordination and Layout: Judith Whipple

Editorial Assistants: Dagny Janss, Margot Kernan,
Marian May, Peggy Park, Dixie Taylor
Design Consultants: Richard Dawson, William Gibson

Special Consultants: Lawrence Clark Powell,
W. W. Robinson, Robert Weinstein

Lane Magazine & Book Company · Menlo Park, California

This book was printed by Times-Mirror Press, Los Angeles, and Peninsula Lithograph
Company, Menlo Park, from lithograph film by Balzer-Shopes Lithoplate Company
Inc.; cover produced by The Cardinal Company; binding by Cardoza Bookbinding
Company. Type composition was done by Atherton's Advertising Typography, Inc.
Paper is Northwest Mountie Enamel and Champion's Garamond Laid Text.

*Cover photographs: Mount Wilson panorama by David Muench, civic center fountains
by Neil Lakata. Title page photograph of Music Center by Baltazar Korab, courtesy
of Welton Becket & Associates. Layout assistance by Joe Seney. Art by Jane Oka.*

THIS IS A PORTRAIT of an extraordinary metropolis: greater Los Angeles—a scattering of communities that has evolved into a great urban complex, unified by ties of social, cultural, and economic interest and laced together by a unique mode of transportation that enables people to pursue far-flung interests with little concern for time or distance—a metropolis built on wheels, dependent on the automobile and benefiting from its mobility.

A city of ceaseless change and innovation, impatient of precedent, inhabited by people who do things on a grand scale, solving problems with flair and imagination, creating a man-made landscape of surprises and contrasts, tending the sophisticated needs of far-out technology.

Benefiting from its unique setting, the Los Angeles plain basks under a mild climate that offers a long year for outdoor work or play.

An abundance of natural wonders, surrounding the metropolitan area, provides quick escape to the solace of the sea, mountains, or desert.

These are the facets of a complicated city, and from them we have chosen to portray a sampling of the sights and customs that Angelenos regard with affection or pride.

Greater Los Angeles: a tapestry of 40 cities spreads over a great plain

MT. WILSON PANORAMA / DAVID MUENCH

between the mountains and the sea, covering an area as large as Rhode Island.

*On the outskirts of
the metropolis
lie the ocean and
mountains, close-in
and accessible,
offering change and
renewal for city dwellers.*

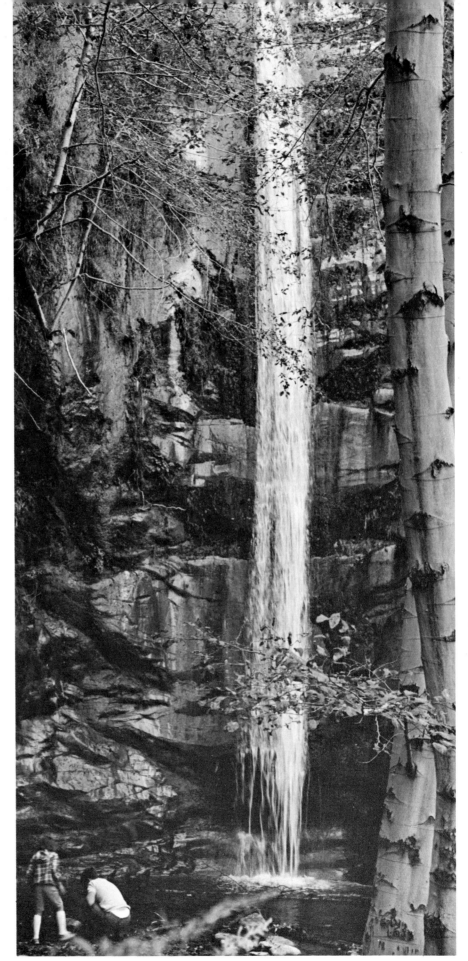

SAN GABRIEL CANYON WATERFALL / WALTER HOUK

HARBOR FREEWAY / DAVID MUENCH

*A city of movement and change, impatient of precedent
and historical tradition, ceaselessly rebuilding.*

DISNEYLAND / BILL TARA

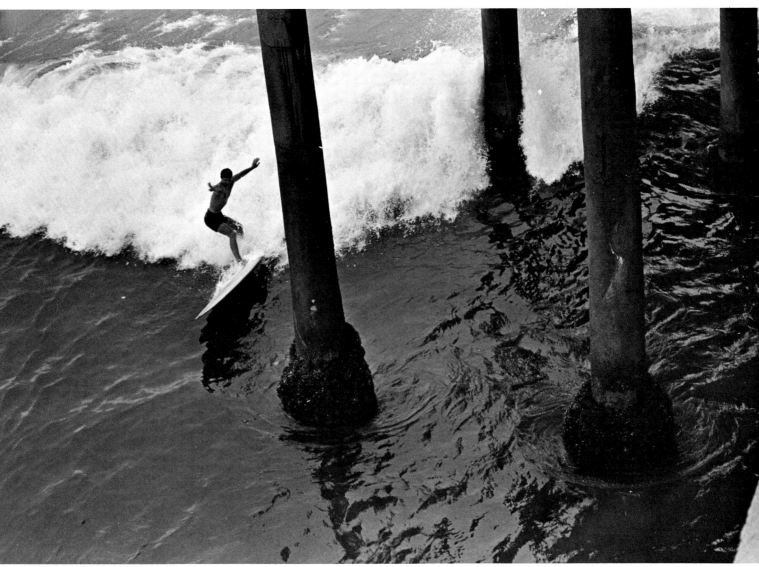

HUNTINGTON BEACH PIER / R. J. SANTIBANEZ

*A lively people, restless and hard-driving even
in play, called by the sun and the sea, bemused by
diversions of incredible variety and style.*

For all to see…
vigorous community
pursuit of cultural
enterprise. Palaces for
the arts, fashioned in
contemporary classical
form, supported by
a profusion of artists
and patrons.

MARK TAPER FORUM / MAURICE MANSON

Contents

APPENDIX

BEGINNINGS
OF A
LIVELY CITY

For nearly two centuries, Los Angeles' natural charms have lured legions of settlers, who, once established, have busily reshaped the landscape to accommodate their needs and aspirations.

A PASTORAL LITTLE PUEBLO, founded in 1781, was never the same again after the Americans seized it in 1848 and launched a tumultuous century of expansion.

On a summer evening in September 1781, a band of foot-sore travelers from Mexico gathered beside a little river to dedicate a settlement that they had trekked 1,000 miles to establish. With appropriate ceremony, they gave it the mouth-filling name of El Pueblo de Nuestra Señora la Reina de Los Angeles de Porciúncula (the town of Our Lady the Queen of the Angels of Porciúncula), which soon became popularly known as El Pueblo and, in time, as Los Angeles.

The founding of the pueblo was part of a last-ditch scheme by the king of Spain to colonize California, remotest of outposts, to protect it from seizure by czarist Russians moving down from Alaska. Padres from New Spain (Mexico), who preceded the colonists by a dozen years, founded missions at San Diego in 1769 and San Gabriel in 1771, Christianized the Indians and trained them in crafts. The new pueblo was planned to supplement the production of the missions and to reduce the need for importing foodstuffs to support the colony, and it soon was producing almost as much as Mission San Gabriel, by then a prodigious agricultural success.

In an action that had far-reaching consequences for a century to come, the provincial governor in 1784 awarded grazing lands to three veterans of the army of occupation, and set a pattern to be followed by subsequent governors who gave away nearly all of California in a patchwork of vast landholdings. Cattle replaced farm produce as the principal source of wealth. As demand grew for hides and tallow to trade with New England vessels that began to visit the coast, "Yankee banknotes," as the stiff hides were called, flowed east in exchange for luxuries for the isolated Californians. For several golden decades the rancheros lived a life of gracious ease.

It was too good to last. Yankee sailors boasted about the coastal paradise when they returned to Boston. A few American explorers and trappers found their way into the province, where, if they were not imprisoned or expelled, they married senoritas and stayed on. Authorities were unable to stem the inflow of Americans and became even less able to cope with it after a revolution in Mexico in 1822 severed connections with Spain and threw the territory into political turmoil that lasted for twenty-five years.

Wracked with dissension, California was ripe for seizure by the first military power to reach it. American army scouts and war vessels began to appear, and by the time the war between the United States and Mexico had broken out in 1846, American forces were already in the province or waiting on the outskirts. The Californians put up a spirited defense and kept American troops out of Southern California for two months before capitulating. In 1848, the area was ceded to the United States by the treaty ending the war, and Los Angeles became an American city.

After the Americans took over, the town changed slowly—mostly for the worse. Isolated from the rest of the United States by mountain and desert barriers and apparently unblessed by anything more than climate, it attracted few settlers. Of the thousands of gold seekers who poured into northern California in the Gold Rush only a small fraction came south—and most of them were fugitives from vigilantes. In 1850,

Los Angeles had a population of 1,610, San Francisco, 35,000. Ten years later, the figures were respectively 4,400 and 57,000.

For a sorry decade, Los Angeles — or Los Diablos as it was known in some quarters — echoed to gunfire and violence, spawned by an unsavory blend of renegades from the north, dispossessed mission Indians, mustered-out soldiers, and unemployed cowhands, thrown out of work by drought and the collapse of the market for beef.

A few hardy pioneers, unperturbed by the uproar around them, quietly went about setting up businesses, planting orchards, vineyards, and wheat on land acquired from Mexican landowners. In time, as the crops matured, business leaders saw the need for getting connections with the outside world. When the transcontinental railroad reached San Francisco in 1869, an effort was made to lure it south, but a Southern Pacific research team reported that Los Angeles was too unpromising to warrant rail connections. Local leaders finally persuaded the company to bring its tracks to town by paying a heavy subsidy in cash, land, and the gift of a small railroad.

Arrival of the Southern Pacific in 1876, followed nine years later by the Santa Fe, emphatically ended Los Angeles' isolation. The two lines launched a rate war that drew settlers by the tens of thousands in one of the great migrations of history. To lure passengers, the railroads reduced fares and trumpeted the virtues of living in California — "The Italy of America" — in a massive advertising campaign. In a train trip that was comparable to an ocean voyage in duration, 130,000 immigrants poured into the area in 15 years. Mostly people with some means, many already held land options, but the rest were taken quickly in hand by silver-tongued salesmen who sold off thousands of real and imaginary townsites. The land rush reached a peak in 1888, then collapsed.

Somehow, a few solid little towns took root, businesses survived, and the fruits of the land began to fill the marketplace. Los Angeles was settling comfortably into an agrarian community — when an unexpected turn sent it permanently down the path toward industrialization.

Wildcat oil prospectors drilling in downtown Los Angeles brought in a producing well in 1892 and triggered an oil fever that changed the face of the city. Derricks sprouted in lawns and backyards and thousands forested the hills to the west. The black wealth gushing out of the ground soon glutted the market, and the industry suffered a series of booms and busts before it finally settled down to a steady output, given a welcome boost by the appearance of a new customer: the insatiable motor car.

From the start, the automobile and Los Angeles seemed made for each other. The long distances, a flat terrain that held no terrors for the under-powered cars of the day, and a mild climate that permitted operation through the winter combined to make an ideal habitat for horseless carriages, and they multiplied luxuriantly. As early as 1905, a magazine writer was able to report that "more automobiles are to be found here than in any other community of like population in America," and by 1916, there were 55,000 cars in the county (one for every 13 persons). Along with the proliferation of the automobile, a flowering of the electric railway lines spread an early form of rapid transit over the region and, between the two of them, car and trolley made all areas accessible and stimulated the area's sprawling growth.

Industries began to appear, attracted by the clean fuel, availability of open space, presence of a tractable labor force, and the gentle climate that permitted year-round production without shutdowns for snow or ice. Industrial growth was leisurely up to World War II, when it exploded under the impact of war needs. After the war, the area found itself to be a major manufacturing center, producing in incredible variety.

THE FIRST SETTLERS felt at home in this dry land

Outpost of Imperial Spain

A handful of men a world away from home built the Los Angeles pueblo, lived comfortably off the land and fruits of Indian labor for seven leisurely decades.

LUCKIER THAN SOME OF THEIR compatriots, the first families of
Los Angeles arrived safely at the site of their future home in 1781
at the end of a 1,000-mile, seven-month journey from northern Mexico.
Six weeks earlier, a second party of colonists for the new pueblo,
following a different route, had been attacked by Indians, some of
the men massacred, women and children taken captive. Recruited from
farming communities in the arid northern provinces, the eleven families
were used to farming in a dry land, and they soon had flourishing crops
growing along the banks of the off-and-on river with the flowing
name: El Río de Nuestra Señora la Reina de Los Angeles de Porciúncula.

SOLDIERS LED the
Spanish overland parties;
sometimes wore medieval
armor, such as this hot and
heavy helmet.

23

COMPLETE CITIES IN THEMSELVES,
the missions were self-sustaining units in the
Spanish colonial scheme that depended on
vast acreages for crops and pasturage.
Mission San Gabriel (1771), one of the
largest and the fourth in the California
chain, covered many acres with its shops,
living quarters, granaries, and chapels. In
its final year of operation, it sheltered 1,300
Indians, produced 12,000 tons of field crops,
and herded 26,000 head of livestock, which
grazed over several hundred square miles
of mission-owned range. Crossroad of several
trails, it was a waypoint for travelers —
notably, Jedediah Strong Smith (LEFT), first
of several million Americans to enter
California from the east.

PLENTIFUL WATER was a life-or-death necessity to
the missions built in a land of little rain, and great
ingenuity was used in diverting it from rivers and springs
to the mission compound. Some was used for irrigation,
some in cooking and tanning, and some was released
in open-air laundries, such as this Moorish fountain
at San Fernando.

JOHN S. WEIR

THOUSANDS OF LONGHORNS ranged the wide valleys

QUICK, UNEASY, AND RESTLESS, prone to attack an unmounted man, the wild descendants of the few hundred head brought north by the first settlers roamed the Los Angeles plains in vast herds throughout the first half of the last century. The stock belonged to the missions and a handful of rancheros and was sorted out once a year at colorful rodeos. A growing market for hides and tallow made cattle raising the major source of wealth, trade, food, and employment until well after the Gold Rush. Headquarters of this booming business was the pueblo of Los Angeles, "Queen of the Cow Country."

27

HOMES FROM THE SOIL for a proud people

TRANSPLANTED FROM SPAIN, the houses built by the Spanish and Mexican colonists in the early 1800's were uniquely suited to the Mediterranean climate of Los Angeles. Thick-walled, shaded by wide verandas, and formed around a patio, the Spanish farmhouse was so well adapted to local needs that it is still being copied in home design. The first drafty adobes had no hung windows and doors and were roofed with tarred reeds. Later versions were graced with conveniences brought by trading vessels and embellishments introduced by wandering Yankee carpenters. Of the few score adobes still standing, Los Cerritos (1837) in Long Beach (ABOVE) is one of the best preserved and most inviting.

HOLDING THEIR breath for an itinerant
photographer, a group of rancheros reveals
in their dress and poise the prosperity and
self-confidence that characterized life in the
ranch houses during two golden decades,
when demand was high for tallow, hides, and
beef. A gay and easygoing social life
revolved around weddings and christenings,
balls and barbecues, and frequent rodeos.

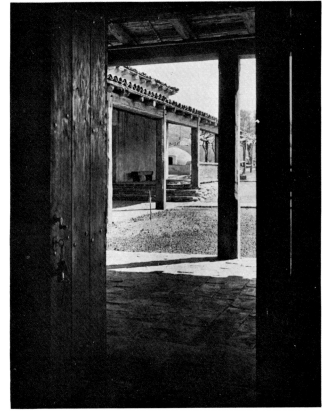

TIMBER AND SOIL on the site were used
to build the adobes, following simple
construction practices used for centuries in
Spain. Timbers were lashed together with
rawhide or held with pegs. Walls, formed of
sun-dried adobe blocks, dissolved in the rain
unless protected by a water-tight roof
and wide eaves.

EL PUEBLO, the Queen of the Cow Country

PLAZA CHURCH, the spiritual heart of the pueblo, was built in 1822 with proceeds from sale of seven barrels of mission brandy to benefit parishioners weary of trudging eight miles to Mission San Gabriel for Sunday services. The setting for a lively calendar of fiestas, christenings, weddings, and holiday playlets, the church still stands, drastically modernized, and its ancient bells still toll out the Angelus as they have since the founding.

FLAT-ROOFED ADOBE PUEBLO was social and trading center for the ranchos, state capital for two years. Dusty lanes, radiating in all directions from the pueblo, followed lines of least resistance, eventually became base of much of present street and highway system.

BULL AND BEAR fights, cockfights, and horse races raised the dust on the Plaza on Sundays; liquor shops and monte parlors around the edge kept the alcalde hopping.

GENERAL PICO won the battles, but lost the war

*HARD-RIDING RANCHEROS, led by General Andrés Pico (*LEFT*) held American troops at bay in Southern California for several months after California had been declared a prize of war by Commodore Sloat in Monterey, July 7, 1846. At home in the saddle and familiar with terrain, the* Californios, *armed with lances and* reatas *were able to out-ride and out-fox the American forces. Pico's men forced the U. S. Army out of Los Angeles in September, inflicted a bloody defeat on a relief column at San Pasqual back of San Diego in December, and kept possession of all Southern California until January of the following year.*

L.A. CO. MUSEUM OF NATURAL HISTORY

BEGINNING OF THE END at the Battle of San Gabriel River (January 8, 1847), as pictured above by an excitable artist with the U. S. Navy, saw a force of 600 Californios give way before an equal array of American troops. Although the Mexican lancers regrouped next day for a final skirmish at La Mesa (site of the present stockyards), they were routed by the Americans and General Pico surrendered four days later. American forces moved back to Los Angeles and set up a provisional government, but the pueblo did not become a legal adjunct to the United States until a year later when the treaty of Guadalupe Hidalgo ended the Mexican War and ceded California to the Union.

Makings of a Metropolis

In one of history's heaviest migrations, Americans poured into Los Angeles, swamped the Latin culture, revamped the landscape, and improvised a great metropolis.

RAILROADS REACH the city, bring settlers by the trainload

BRASS BAND welcomed the Santa Fe in 1885 when it arrived in Los Angeles—a city the line really had never planned to serve. Once established, the railroad fought the Southern Pacific, already on the scene, for transcontinental passengers in a rate war that reduced fares from Missouri from $100 to $25 and, for a day or so, an incredible $1. The two railroads brought hundreds of thousands of settlers, many with land options purchased with their tickets.

CROSSING THE MOUNTAIN barrier north of Los Angeles in the 1870's was as tough an engineering problem as crossing the Sierra had been a few years before. In a crow-flight distance of 14 miles, tracks had to ascend half a mile, a real challenge for the short-winded locomotives of the day. Brilliantly engineered, the Southern Pacific line was blasted through 17 tunnels and curved around the spectacular Tehachapi Loop where it made a complete circle.

MAKINGS OF A METROPOLIS   35

CLIMATE FOR SALE! Come and get it, everybody!

"A MID-WINTER'S day outing" in 1897 by the directors of the august Pasadena Board of Trade proved photographically that tall tales about the climate were really true. The energetic group made their trip in an elapsed time that would be hard to equal today:

"10:15 a.m. — Refreshments, oranges"

"11:30 a.m. — Frolic in the snow"

"3:30 p.m. — Bath at Santa Monica"

CALIFORNIA HISTORICAL SOCIETY

MODESTY WAS HARDLY the main virtue of the railroad posters that flowered all over the nation and abroad from 1880's on, causing a stampede of settlers eager for a stake in paradise.

CALIFORNIA
The Cornucopia of the World
ROOM
FOR
MILLIONS
OF
IMMIGRANTS

43.795.000.
ACRES
OF GOVERNMENT LANDS
UNTAKEN

Railroad & Private Land for a Million Farmers
A Climate for Health & Wealth WITHOUT CYCLONES
OR BLIZZARDS

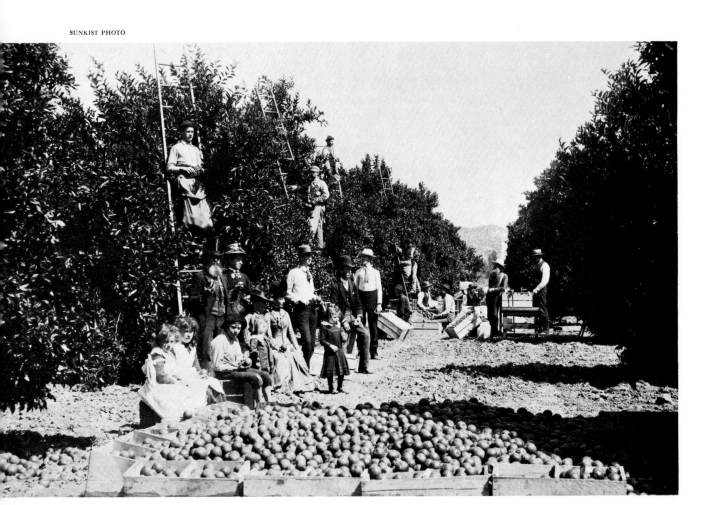

AN AIR OF GENTILITY pervaded the orange industry from the start. Growing oranges — described as "not only a fruit but a romance"— attracted wealthy men out of retirement to come West and put their capital and experience to work in the groves. The urban-rural aristocracy which they formed is typified by the Sunday-best group above, posing unconvincingly as pickers and packers.

INTRODUCED TO eliminate the "absurdity of hand grading," the California Fruit Grader was advertised in the 1890's as having "made as great a revolution in the fruit business as the elevator has in architecture."

FROM THIS NEATLY manicured grove, planted on a former rancho near the pueblo, the first rail shipment of California oranges was sent to St. Louis in 1877. The trip took a month but the fruit arrived "tired but intact," and proved the feasibility of shipping to distant points. These oranges were from trees descended from the original orchard set out at San Gabriel Mission in 1804. The Padres had been well aware that this Mediterranean fruit would thrive in California, and had experimented at Mission Ventura 30 years earlier. The initial mission stock was displaced in the 1870's by navel oranges introduced from Brazil, and from such humble beginnings grew a huge industry that ultimately lured more settlers than the Gold Rush.

BOOM TOWNS of the 1880's—
the best survived the frenzy

FEW OF THE INLAND boom towns were as well planned as Ontario (1883), with its stately divided boulevard stretching to the mountains, a pleasant sight that has survived to the present day. Promoted with the usual razzle dazzle, the town was conceived carefully and it grew solidly. As with many boom towns, provision was made for a college, which actually came into being as a branch of USC (it is now a junior college). One of the quaint sights of the town was the gravity streetcar that ran down the long boulevard. Mules pulled the cars to the top, then gravely mounted a platform on the rear, and coasted down to the bottom.

UNBLUSHING
promotion was the order
of the day in ads placed in
newspapers and magazines.

LAND SALE AT MONROVIA (1886) was typical of
the frenzied 1880's, when brass bands, free meals, circus
performers, and free excursions were used to attract
buyers. Monrovia grew into a stable community, but not
all the boom towns survived. Land sharks lured the
susceptible to townsites in river beds (promoted as farm
land), on steep hillsides (view lots), in the desert (health
resort), swamp lands (harbor). Oversold, real estate
collapsed in a cascade of paper profits. Of the
hundred-odd towns plotted between 1884–90, 62
vanished without a trace.

41

BIG RED CARS, singing trolleys to everywhere

"THE GREATEST ELECTRIC RAILWAY system on earth" was the claim of the Pacific Electric, which in its heyday (1920's) covered 1,200 miles of track that laced the entire Los Angeles plain from shore to mountain (ABOVE). Originally developed in 1901 as a real estate promotion by Henry E. Huntington, the system was designed to open suburban areas not reached by public transportation. Between 1902-07, rails were laid in all directions, often years ahead of population, giving a tremendous impetus to sprawling growth. Inland boom towns of the 1880's, such as Sierra Madre (RIGHT), boomed all over again when the rails reached them after 1906. Service was frequent and fast (as the circle on the map indicates), and it was possible to reach some areas quicker during the rush hour by trolley than it is today by freeway.

EACH CONDUCTOR had his own individual punch mark; more than eleven hundred different designs were used by PE.

DONALD DUKE

42

SEASHORE CITIES had a tang all their own

GENUINE VENETIAN GONDOLIERS poled their way through the canals of Venice-by-the-Sea, fanciest of all shoreline developments, brainchild of a wealthy easterner, Abbot Kinney, who had made a fortune from Sweet Caporal cigarettes. Well-educated, world-traveled Kinney built his dream city in 1905 from 160 acres of sand dunes and salt marsh, with homes, hotels, interconnecting canals plied by a fleet of gondolas, amusement halls, and a large Chautauqua auditorium. Unfortunately, oil developments ruined the area, and only a few bridges and weed-grown canals remain today.

THE MILE OF HONKY-TONK amusements along the Long Beach Pike offered startling contrast to the staid character of the city, founded in the 1880's by sober middlewesterners as "an educational watering place" where, along with dancing and card playing, "objectionable or inappropriate bathing suits" were prohibited. Built in late 1800's, the Pike had changed little when this photograph was taken in 1900 — indeed, much of it looks the same even today.

THE ROBUST PLEASURES of the
seashore drew throngs to the beach

"ALL THE WONDERFUL vegetable and animal life in the bottom of the ocean" could be seen through the glass bottom of the sidewheeler Cleopatra that circled above the Under Sea Gardens off Catalina Island.

"THE FROLICSOME OLD OCEAN," as it was described in an early brochure, attracted Angelenos by the hundreds as one beach after another was made accessible by trolley lines. In the early 1900's, the green cars of the Los Angeles Pacific Railway rocketed Sunday bathers from downtown Los Angeles to the surf at Venice (LEFT) in 35 minutes.

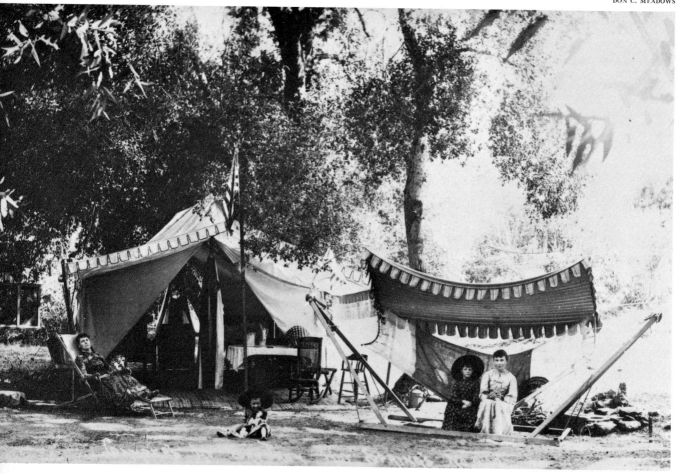

THE CAMPING CRAZE started early, as Angelenos domesticated the mountains around them. The comfortable family above was photographed in the 1890's in the Santa Ana Mountains, where nearly every canyon had a dozen campsites. In the 1860's, hikers had camped on the heights of the San Gabriels and San Jacintos and, by 1870, orderly tent resorts had begun to appear along the primitive mountain roads.

LEGENDARY MT. LOWE RAILWAY, a breathtaking conquest of the San Gabriels by trolley and cable car in 1892, was the brainchild of a Civil War balloonist named Thaddeus Sobreski Coulincourt Lowe. A trolley line ran from Pasadena to the base of the mountains, where passengers transferred to a cable incline that hoisted them up a 62 per cent grade (LEFT) to a station where they again transferred to another trolley that twisted among the conifers amid an occasional snow storm (RIGHT) — to reach a cluster of hotels at the summit. Absorbed by the Pacific Electric, the railway was popular for four decades, went out of business in 1936 when the tavern burned to the ground.

UNDER SUNNY SKIES
poppies and oranges flourished

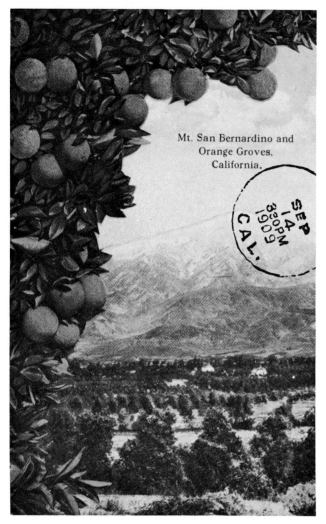

Mt. San Bernardino and
Orange Groves,
California.

SEP
14
3:30PM
1909
CAL.

IMMORTAL CLICHE: this idyllic scene of oranges ripening against a backdrop of snow-capped mountains has appealed to tourists and promoters alike for three generations. The oranges-in-winter postcard — a best-seller from the start — is still popular with visitors to the citrus belt.

CALIFORNIA POPPIES by the square mile carpeted the plains of Los Angeles every spring. The dazzling spectacle captivated all who saw it and many, such as the dapper group at the right, took trolley excursions to the wildflower fields behind Altadena in the early 1900's.

WORLD PORT scooped from mudflats

HARBINGER OF THE FUTURE, Teddy Roosevelt's Great White Fleet rides at anchor near the new port that would later become a major naval base. The 16 snowy, glistening ships, welcomed with week-long festivities, were on the last leg of a round-the-world voyage, dispatched by the President to impress other nations with this country's might.

SEVERAL THOUSAND TONS of Santa Catalina Island were barged across the open sea to form a long breakwater that changed the mudflats off San Pedro into a world port. The first bargeload of rock, dumped into the ocean in 1899, signaled the end of a bitter, eight-year feud between San Pedro and Santa Monica over the future port. The big splash was celebrated by a jubilee and a flag-bedecked barbecue attended by 20,000 people. The protective barrier, which eventually stretched nine miles, supplanted an earlier one, built in the 1870's by an army of wheelbarrowers.

SHOESTRING TO tidewater. Los Angeles had to reach a long way for a port. The Spanish founders had planned for an inland farming community with no need for a harbor. Thus, when the city was ready for ocean commerce a century later, it had to stretch 30 miles to the sea. The unique "Shoestring," annexed in 1906, brought the harbor into the city limits and legalized the spending of municipal funds on essential port development.

December 25, 1906

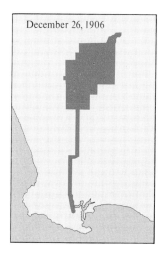

December 26, 1906

FROM PUEBLO to metropolis in 50 years

SPREAD ALL OVER the map by 1900, as shown in this photo taken from the base of Mount Wilson, Los Angeles was reaching out in all directions. Towns, subdivisions, and orange groves covered flat land that years before had been empty except for herds of longhorn cattle.

FIRST OFFICIAL MAP (1849) of the city shows street names in both Spanish and English and reveals the unique orientation of the town to a NE-SW pattern instead of the cardinal points. Later real estate developments were laid out true to the compass, thus creating jogs and bends in the streets wherever the new plats butted up against the original pueblo.

IN A SCANT 50 years, Los Angeles exploded from a little pueblo of 1,600 in 1850 to a major metropolis of 100,000 souls — of whom 90 per cent had arrived since 1880, lured by visions of economic opportunity in a Mediterranean paradise. Baedeker noted approvingly in his guide book for 1900 that the adobes had "given place almost entirely to stone and brick business blocks and tasteful wooden residences." So rapid was the growth of the business district that it acquired an architectural consistency — captured in this conscientious drawing of 1900 — that gave Downtown a turn-of-the-century air that persisted for decades.

TWO VENERABLE landmarks
turn back the clock to
Los Angeles' gilded age

"WORLD'S SHORTEST RAILWAY", Angel's Flight
ascends the steep slope of Bunker Hill, as it has done
since 1901 when it was built to serve the wealthy
residents whose homes were clustered on the summit and
later to carry tourists to the 100-foot observation tower
that offered a view of the San Gabriel Mountains. The
tower is gone, and so are the mansions — razed to make
way for urban renewal — but the little orange cars still
clack their way up and down, offering a heady shot of
nostalgia for only 5¢.

OF THE TURN-OF-THE-CENTURY business
buildings still left, none attracts more attention than the
astonishing Bradbury Building, designed in 1893 by
George H. Wyman, a designer who never again
equaled this virtuoso performance. The plain façade of
the building does not prepare the visitor for the
exhilarating interior — a bold blend of the cast iron
curlicues of its era with an airy use of space and sunlight
that anticipated later architectural thinking.

THE BLACK BONANZA that transformed Los Angeles

"WELLS AS THICK as holes in a pepperpot" appeared overnight in 1890's after oil-pioneer Edward L. Doheny dug a hole with pick and shovel near Second and Glendale and brought in a producing well at 46 feet. Downtown, hundreds of derricks soon crowded residential area (ABOVE) now occupied by the freeway interchange known as the Stack. (Many of the wells are still pumping in basements and backyards; on warm nights, the scent of petroleum gas pervades the air.) Within 6 years, 3,000 wells were crammed into a 4-mile strip of western Los Angeles, and the market became glutted with oil. Conversion of locomotives and industrial furnaces from coal to oil and timely arrival of the automobile rescued the industry and started Los Angeles' industrialization.

UNDERGROUND WEALTH revealed itself in seepage at La Brea tarpits, present site of the majestic Los Angeles Art Museum. Seeps were first reported by Spaniards in 1770, brea was used to waterproof roofs of pueblo, and wildcat wells were drilled in 1880's, followed by a producing field in 1900's. Oilmen noticed odd-shaped bones in the ooze, turned area over to scientists who found it to be one of world's richest fossil caches (see p. 176).

WATER FROM
234 miles away

COMPLETELY DEPENDENT on imported water, semi-desert Los Angeles, with only .06 per cent of the natural stream flow in the state, has had to reach out three times to far-away sources. First was the famous Owens River Aqueduct (1907–1913) that diverted the river in the Sierra to the outskirts of Los Angeles. Ebullient fountain (RIGHT) honors William Mulholland, mastermind of the system. Arrival of the water in 1913 was celebrated (BELOW) at the spillway near San Fernando Pass, where thousands witnessed the opening of floodgates.

BY PIPELINE and ditch, the $25 million aqueduct brought water by gravity 234 miles across mountains, canyons, deserts. It was rated second only to Panama Canal as an engineering feat.

MAKINGS OF A METROPOLIS 61

THE MOVIES chose Hollywood
for sun, space, scenery

REVELERS FOR BELSHAZZAR'S FEAST fill out an opulent set built in 1916 for the filming of D. W. Griffith's "Intolerance," one of the earliest of the Hollywood spectaculars. The huge set, shown under construction below, loomed above Sunset Boulevard for years after the film was released. Although an astounding achievement for its day, the 13-reel, $2 million film was a financial failure. Essentially a pacifist story, it was received coolly during the years of World War I. Griffith was one of the greatest of the early producers attracted to Hollywood by its perpetual sunshine, boundless open space, and nearness to seashore, desert, and mountain scenery.

JUMPING GIRL was one of a series of photographic studies of people and animals in motion filmed in California 40 years before Hollywood by pioneer photographer Eadward Muybridge. Forerunner of the present motion picture, the sequences were taken by a line of cameras activated by tripwires.

HIGH FLYING industry from spruce and canvas

BUSY CREW OF TINKERERS, working in the loft of a planing mill in 1920, piece together the plane that launched the mammoth aircraft industry in Los Angeles. First plane in history to airlift a useful load equal to its own weight, the Cloudster was the creation of Donald Douglas (second from left, top), an aeronautical engineer who had started his own business with $600 in an office behind a Santa Monica barber shop. Within three years, Douglas planes had circled the globe in a history-making flight, and other manufacturers were at work in the area. Plane makers were attracted by the benign climate, which permitted fabricating and storing planes outdoors and year-round flight testing, and by the ample pasturage then available for fields and factory expansion.

A WHIMSICAL ARRAY of aircraft filled the sky above Dominguez Field in January 1910 in the first international air meet in the United States. Small dirigible was made to rise or descend by the pilot's walking to the tail or the front of the gangway suspended from the craft.

ROADS BROKE through the mountain barrier

SECURITY FIRST NATIONAL BANK

CAMPING IN STYLE on Cahuenga Pass in 1892, a family cooks lunch while a freighting party stops to gawk. Cahuenga has been a heavily traveled throughway since Indian days, providing passage over the mountain barrier separating San Fernando Valley from the Los Angeles plain. Now reshaped as the Hollywood Freeway, the road at one time followed the typical course of the so-called "passes" over the Santa Monicas. In the absence of a natural cleft through the mountain mass, the half dozen grades follow long canyons up the southern slope to the summit; then, avoiding the steep northern canyons, twist down the face of the mountains.

STAGECOACH ROUTES faced tough going through the mountains. Soldiers sliced a deep cut into the mountain crest near Newhall (1859) to eliminate a precipitous grade. Beale's Cut (LEFT) was used for decades, is still visible to inquisitive tourists.

CORKSCREW RIDGE ROUTE, engineering marvel of 1916, was for 20 years the major highway to the Central Valley. The notorious road twisted and looped for 30 miles along the backbone of Castaic Ridge, a grueling test for tires, gears, steering mechanisms, and radiators. No one who drove it would ever forget it. More than just a highway, the road was considered a means for unifying the state and discouraging agitation for statehood for Southern California. Now a freeway, the highway is still regarded as the most important single road uniting the two Californias.

WALTER HOUK

AUTOMOBILE CLUB OF SOUTHERN CALIFORNIA

67

*A PASSION FOR SPEED manifested itself early in a
rash of road and track races spanning two decades.
First race (1903) was run on sulky track in Agriculture
(Exposition) Park; best-known, the Vanderbilt Cup
competitions in Santa Monica, 1912–16. At Ascot
Speedway (ABOVE), Stutz 8 starts on next-to-last race
(1919) in its 6-year winning career. Racer is today
displayed in Exposition Park.*

*BANDED TOGETHER to wrest some rights
from the horse, 10 beleaguered motorists in
1900 founded a touring club, the
now-influential Automobile Club of Southern
California. By 1909 it had 1,000 members
and its own journal,* Touring Topics *(now*
Westways*). The club issued atlases (1910)
and licenses (1911), posted thousands of road
signs (1907), instituted car insurance (1912)
and roadside service (1918). Champion of
better roads, uniform traffic laws (1920),
outlawing of speed traps (1923).*

PORTENT OF THINGS TO COME, *motorists mass for opening of Mulholland Highway in 1923. By 1928, Los Angeles had one automobile for every 2.25 persons. At present, 40 per cent of state's cars are in the county — only six states have more.*

PEOPLE ON THE MOVE

Like their restless predecessors, today's Angelenos vigorously pursue the good life in an evolving city, keeping much of the past while advancing the frontiers of technology, widening cultural horizons.

No one who has ever flown into Los Angeles on a clear night can forget the overwhelming sight of the great city spread out below — an ocean of twinkling jewels, dazzling even at 5,000 feet — that sweeps to the limits of vision.

As the plane glides down to a landing, the mass of lights takes on individuality and the whole area seems to be in motion. Signals and signs blink on and off, searchlights probe the sky, and streamers of car lights intersect in a precision ballet or roll along the freeways in an endless parade. Long before the plane touches down, the traveler is aware that he is entering a powerful and dynamic city.

It is a restless city, filled with people on the move. A place where buildings are razed, replaced, and razed again; where families move from home to home, shifting base on an average of once every five years. Perpetually renewed by an influx of immigrants, the city changes with the character of each new wave. For 60 years, the population of Los Angeles doubled every census, and now the number of residents in the metropolitan area is second only to New York. People are still coming — most of them from the north central states and the south, with Texans leading the procession — but for the first time the principal growth now comes from within, with natural increase exceeding in-migration. The population is getting younger every year — 40 per cent of the residents are between the ages of 20 and 49 (above the national average) and only 8.7 per cent are past retirement age (below the national average).

This is a city with an incredible talent pool — in all the arts and especially all the performing arts. More serious music can be heard every day in Los Angeles than in either New York or London. Here is home for Artur Rubinstein, Igor Stravinsky, Gregor Piatigorsky, Ruth St. Denis, and Jascha Heifetz. A receptive public supports a vigorous musical program and an inventive theater, performing in culture palaces, staffed by artists from the motion pictures, television, and radio industries.

Here also is talent in the sciences, teaching at Caltech, brainstorming at the Rand Corporation, plotting our actions after the moon landing, predicting the aftermath of nuclear holocaust. Few metropolitan areas can match the profusion of highly ranked colleges and universities, libraries and scientific museums scattered over this area. Nor can many equal the variety and quantity of the art galleries and the quality of the art on display.

Angelenos can amuse themselves with a wide choice of diversions, thanks to their own mobility and the shirt-sleeve climate. Spectator or participator, the sports fan can find plenty to stir the blood. The Los Angeles Dodgers draw the biggest box office in professional baseball, playing in what may be the best outdoor theater built since Ephesus. In a summer month, a quarter of a million golfers compete for starting times on the public courses and five million sunworshippers take to the beaches. In winter, hardy ones are out there just the same but the number drops respectively to 170,000 and 250,000. Skiers and surfers divide their year between the mountains and the sea, or take off nonchalantly on a 700-mile round-trip for a weekend of skiing in the Sierra or surfing off Mexico.

Behind all this activity is a vigorous economy, built around a manufacturing industry of great diversity. A relative newcomer as a major manufacturing center, Los Angeles has enjoyed untold benefits from its late start. With no locked-in industrial traditions to buck, businessmen have been free to try the unknown, innovate new processes and introduce new products. There is adventure in the air, and it is no coincidence that some of the major industries here were started as outrageous gambles. In how many cities would bankers unlock their vaults to bet on wildcat oil wells, flying machines, nickelodeons, and, in recent memory, rockets? This innovative attitude, basically a "why not" approach, has led the region to its highly diversified development.

The metropolitan area leads the nation in aircraft production, electronics, gasoline service stations, automobile sales, canned seafood, dairy production, and armaments. It is second in the country in the number of telephones, in manufacture of scientific instruments, and expenditures for books, records, entertainment, and sporting goods. It stands third in wholesale sale of alcoholic beverages.

Much of the local economy revolves around the automobile, the indispensable family member, distributed one for every 2.2 persons. Los Angeles County has more motor vehicles than all but a few states and consumes $1 billion worth of gasoline a year. Angelenos pay out $3 billion a year on new cars, $100 million on car and truck rentals. According to opinion pollsters, Angelenos are fond of their freeways—except when jammed at rush hour or immobilized by fog or, as has happened, by spilled molasses, BB shot, or Herefords. There are 2,500 tow trucks registered in the county, and the record for the world's greatest collision is still held by the Santa Ana Freeway, where 224 cars piled into each other because of one flat tire.

Although it is fashionable to decry Los Angeles as a headless monster unable to plan its own future, let alone cope with its present, there is a surprising amount of communal force that makes for cohesive and unified action. For one thing, the enormous size and spread of the city, plus its jigsaw shape that fits it in and around other civic atolls, enforces a kind of regional planning by the sheer weight and intimacy of the city's embrace. Los Angeles County fills in the remaining open spaces, works closely with small cities, and cooperates with the surrounding counties. On top of it all, a conglomerate of regional and cross-jurisdictional agencies share enough common interests to pull together in relative harmony. Indeed, the accomplishments of "planless" Los Angeles are the envy of many metropolitan areas of comparable size that are hamstrung by the pride and jealousy of contiguous cities and counties.

Problems that boggle the imagination by their scope and complexity are coolly taken in stride. While other cities debate airport crowding, Los Angeles' planners develop solutions a decade ahead, and construction is started on the airport of the future. While other cities battle highway engineers, the wheeled citizenry of this area accept the freeways as a way of life and support a proliferation of highways that keeps better pace with the growing car population than other areas strangling for lack of roads. Although the pall of smog is the price Angelenos pay for their mobile ways, the blight is under attack in the laboratory and steps are being taken to reduce or finally dispel it. As available flatlands disappear from the real estate market, buildings begin to climb skyward, but they are held in check by sensible limits on height and groundspace to forestall creation of urban canyons or overloading neighborhoods with cars and people.

And so it goes. Of course not every urban problem is being solved well or in time — it is easy to tick off a score of unsolved problems or wretched solutions — but the number of good answers is reassuring.

Getting Around in the Urban Maze

*A city on wheels, Los Angeles pioneered the freeway net;
has more cars than it had people in 1940; leans on
the automobile, but takes to the air when things get tight.*

TWO GENERATIONS of freeways in ten years

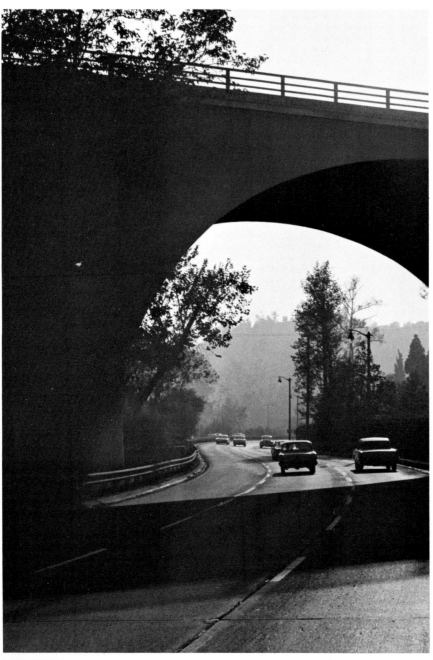

*FIRST FREEWAY in
California and still the most
scenic and pleasant to drive in
off hours, the 8.2-mile stretch
between Los Angeles and
Pasadena opened December
1940 — had its first traffic jam
three days later when Rose
Bowl fans clogged it. Marvel
of its day; now considered too
tight, too curvaceous by
present standards.*

*A NEWER BREED, the
eight-lane swath of the San
Diego Freeway sweeps out of
the mountains, runs straight
as an arrow for miles. It is
arteries such as this that
permit thousands of students
at UCLA (CENTER LEFT) to
commute to class every
school day.*

J. R. EYERMAN

BARON WOLMAN

WHERE EVERY MAN
is his own
transit system

THOUGH DISPERSED over 1,800 square miles, Angelenos circulate freely through the urban maze, traveling long distances to work, or play, and think more in terms of driving time than mileage. Only major city to take form after invention of the motor car, Los Angeles' horizontal growth has been shaped by the car and its people indentured to it. Circulation is facilitated by freeway system, planned to the hilt in 1959. It now covers 350 miles of paving; will stretch to 1,500 by 1980, completion date. Plans call for supplementing the freeway net with an electronically operated rapid transit system in the 1970's formed around eight heavily traveled routes radiating from downtown Los Angeles.

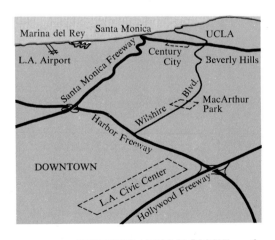

WHEN TRAFFIC IS LIGHT on the freeways, motorists can drive from one end of the Los Angeles Plain to the other in jig time, but during rush hours, cars jammed on the freeways often slow to a crawl. Parking lots, spangled with automobiles, cover one-third of downtown Los Angeles.

PLANNING for the future of the automobile

CALIFORNIA DIVISION OF HIGHWAYS

RESEARCH IN THE WAYS of the automobile progresses on many fronts. A panel of "noise listeners" (ABOVE), stationed on the Ridge Route, evaluates noise level of freeway travel as part of an over-all survey of noise tolerance by the FAA. (LEFT): Plans for future freeways, developed by Division of Highways, foresee depressed green belts passing through residential areas and elevated viaducts, with storage and shops below, traversing commercial districts.

AUTOMOBILE-CONSCIOUS LOS ANGELES passes its tastes along to the rest of the country through prestigious Art Center College, which offers a stiff course in car design. Partially underwritten by major car manufacturers, the curriculum supplies more than half of Detroit's designers.

MAURICE E. MANSON

FREEWAYS channel speeding rivers of cars

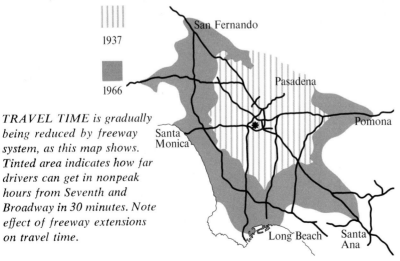

TRAVEL TIME *is gradually being reduced by freeway system, as this map shows. Tinted area indicates how far drivers can get in nonpeak hours from Seventh and Broadway in 30 minutes. Note effect of freeway extensions on travel time.*

1937

1966

San Fernando

Pasadena

Pomona

Santa Monica

Long Beach

Santa Ana

HEART OF THE FREEWAY *system is the much-photographed four-level interchange in downtown Los Angeles. First in the world, it has been studied and photographed ad infinitum since it was opened in the 1950's. Although it safely carries 345,000 vehicles a day, it is outmoded by newer, wide-sweeping interchanges. Engineers now criticize it as too cramped, requiring drivers to make too many decisions too suddenly.*

STREAMERS OF LIGHT, *the commuters sweep along Harbor Freeway past the first of the Bunker Hill skyscrapers on their way home from work — thousands driving 40 to 50 miles each way every working day.*

DAVID MUENCH

MOBILITY'S PRICE—a pall of hydrocarbons

ROBERT C. FRAMPTON

BANE OF THE ANGELENO'S EXISTENCE is smog, a man-made nuisance that is abetted by Nature. Because of the lay of the land, smog-producing agents in automobile and industrial exhausts are trapped at ground level by a lid of warm air (ABOVE), which actually is visible from the mountain crests. Although regarded as a modern inconvenience, smog was first reported here in 1542 by Spanish explorer Juan Rodrigues Cabrillo, who saw smoke from Indian campfires rise a few hundred feet and then level out, obscuring the base of the mountains. He named present San Pedro Bay for this curious phenomenon, calling it "La Bahia de los Fumos."

ANATOMY OF SMOG: Smog-producing chemicals emitted at ground level cannot escape into the atmosphere. Prevailing winds in summer are often too weak (3 m.p.h.) to blow them away, the surrounding mountains contain them, and on top of it all rests a blanket of warm air that prevents the polluted air from rising and holds it captive under the sun's rays, which transform the air-borne chemicals into eye-smarting irritants.

ON EYE-SMARTING DAYS, familiar landmarks vanish in the haze and air pollution control authorities take air samples to determine if a smog alert should be issued, curtailing certain industries and traffic. In the past decade, 24 alerts have been proclaimed, usually during summer months. The smog problem developed here early, likewise the controls; and beleaguered cities all over the world look to local authorities for advice and assistance. Controls are applied at the source, but many wild solutions have been advanced for dispelling smog itself: huge fans to blow it away, tunnels to draw it through the mountains, blowers to force it down sewers and out to sea, cloud seeding, mirrors and heaters to create updrafts.

HEADING OUT TO SEA, a loaded jet takes off from Los Angeles International Airport while freeway traffic tunnels unconcernedly under the runway. Third busiest in the country, in 1967 the terminal handled 470,000 takeoffs and landings, 18 million passengers. To accommodate even more millions, planners are projecting a five-airport scheme to disperse traffic and science-fiction solutions for the glut of passengers, baggage, and parked cars. Envisioned: small metroports in downtown areas, rapid transit lines to major ports, and mobile waiting rooms that will be plucked into the air by giant helicopters and hustled to the airport.

AIRBORNE WAYS of escaping the freeways

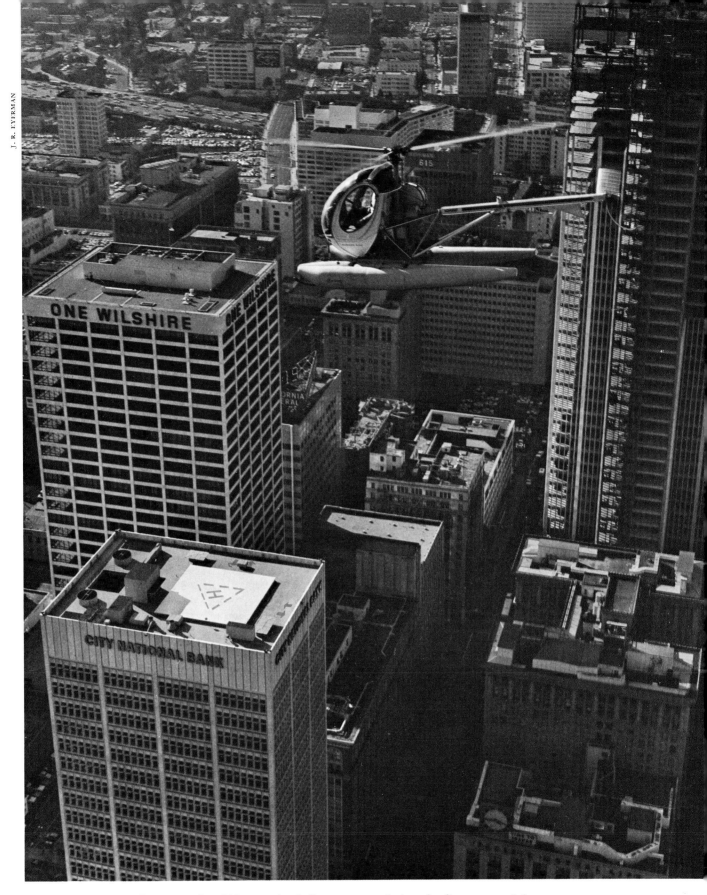

*LIKE A DRAGONFLY, a Hughes 300 executive helicopter comes in for a landing on one of the
20 helipads in downtown Los Angeles. Within the metropolitan area, choppers transport
airline passengers, mail, and civic dignitaries; carry offshore oilmen to and fro; rescue surfers,
capsized boatmen, and fallen hikers. Police use them for directing traffic and race track parking,
even for apprehending car thieves and burglars. They are used in fighting forest fires, re-seeding
burned-over areas, drying soaked crops and orchards.*

85

Exhilaration of Surf and Sea

*Few urban areas offer such a variety of activities
and facilities as the waterworld that stretches
for 100 miles along the Southland's leading edge.*

QUIET PLEASURES of the family beach

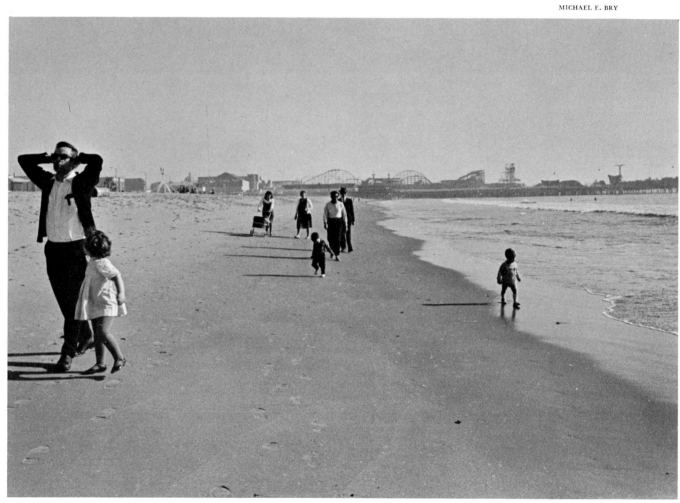

*IN WINTER, USUALLY CROWDED Santa Monica beach is a place of solitude, where
families may leisurely exercise their young and a man can relax in the salty sunshine.
Most popular of area beaches, Santa Monica has been favored since 1860's when
it was only a sheep ranch. The beach today is marching slowly westward, thanks to a breakwater (1934) that dumps a million cubic yards of sand on it every year.*

THE SPECTACLE OF 500 fire rings blazing in a two-mile, double strand is a common sight at Huntington Beach on summer nights. Huntington (named for railroad magnate, donor of the famous library) is one of a dozen beach parks operated by state or county agencies between Newport and Malibu. Mostly confined to the narrow tidal strip, usually immersed at high tide, the beach parks prohibit camping in all but two. The pensive pelican (RIGHT), a frequenter of Southland beaches, is oblivious of interloping people.

PAUL RYAN

THE BEACH—forty-mile-long playground

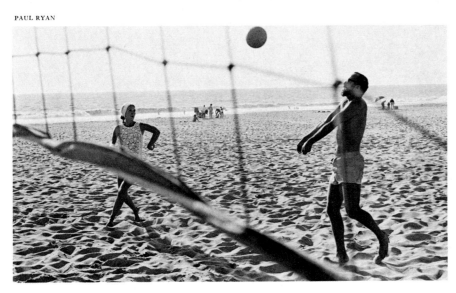

YOUTH TAKES OVER the beaches in summer. Swimmers swarm in the surf, volleyball nets sprout in the sand. Forty miles of life-guarded beach draw 60 million visitors a year. Busiest beach: Santa Monica with 15 million visitors; second, Long Beach with 12 million. Summer Sundays sometimes will attract as many as 125,000 to a popular strand.

WHERE PERMITTED, dune buggies carry the indigenous automania right out into the tidal zone. Marvelously improvised from old cars, the ungainly vehicles are fitted with big bloated tires, can travel freely over sand, either seashore or desert, often winter in Palm Springs area. Banned at most beaches, heavily restricted at others.

SAILS SET for the open sea

HUNDREDS OF SAILS dot the Pacific Ocean during the annual Newport to Ensenada race held in May to coincide with Mexico's Cinco de Mayo celebrations. Ocean-going sailboats from 50 yacht clubs clustered in Newport Harbor, Long Beach, and Marina del Rey, keep busy with a calendar of events that stretches right through the winter. Clubs compete in regattas and races (favorite destination: Catalina and other offshore islands) and participate in festivals, parades, and cruises. Longest races: trans-Pacific runs to Honolulu and South Pacific.

PLEASURE BOATING on sheltered waters

TWIN-HULLED CATAMARAN and a flock of sailing craft of all sizes and contours maneuver in the channel of Marina del Rey on a day of light traffic. On summer weekends the basins are crowded with interweaving craft, and the County's rescue patrol regularly plucks around a dozen capsized sailors from the water. Largest of a half dozen marinas in the area, the complex covers 375 acres of land, 405 of water, has slips for 6,000 boats, provision for 10,000. Shoreside amenities operated on land leased from Los Angeles County include motels, boatels, a shopping center, restaurants, apartments, and a Coast Guard air-sea rescue base.

UNDER A FLAMING summer sunset, moored sailboats await their weekend skippers in a marina in the Los Angeles–Long Beach harbor, where they share the sheltered channels with the U.S. Navy, fishing fleet, and ocean-going vessels. Other marinas are located at Newport Bay, Marina del Rey, Redondo Beach, Alamitos Bay, and Catalina Island. More than 120,000 pleasure craft are registered to owners in Los Angeles and Orange Counties, a third of all the boats in the state.

OFFSHORE ARENA for muscular competition

CREWS FROM *six local colleges race in the sheltered water along the coast. Eight rowers, plus a bantam coxswain, propel the fragile skins of cedar through the water at 10 to 14 miles an hour over a 2,000 meter course. Crews from USC* (LEFT) *and UCLA have qualified for the Olympics and have been able to challenge the long supremacy of Washington and Berkeley in collegiate rowing.*

"LOTTA WATER — PULL THAT BOAT!" sings out the steersman as the 38-foot outrigger plunges through the water on its way from Catalina to Balboa, 26 miles away, in the annual (since 1959) competition between mainland and Hawaiian rowers. The channel between the island and the shore has been traversed by every imaginable conveyance: dories, sail and power boats, water skis, kites, and balloons. It has been swum several times.

WATER SKIERS, cutting furrows through the offshore water, are in such abundance as to make Los Angeles a dominant market for water skis in the country. The sport of water skiing originated in Southern California in the 1930's.

MAINLAND CAPITAL for the Hawaiian sport of kings

PAUL RYAN

THROUGHOUT THE LONG SUMMER, surfers crowd the breakers off a score of beaches between Laguna and County Line, indulging in the 400-year-old royal sport imported from Hawaii, where it was practiced by kings and tribal elite. Some of the gremmies gather in communal herds in the surf off the popular beaches, some practice their solo art alone at dusk after the crowds have gone, and the more adroit enter championship competitions sponsored by beach communities. The crash-helmeted surfer sliding down a moving hill of water at the left is competing for points in the Huntington Beach International. More than 100,000 surfers frequent the area in summer, making it the mainland capital of the sport and underwriting a flourishing surfboard manufacturing industry.

SALTY ART of ocean fishing, ashore and afloat

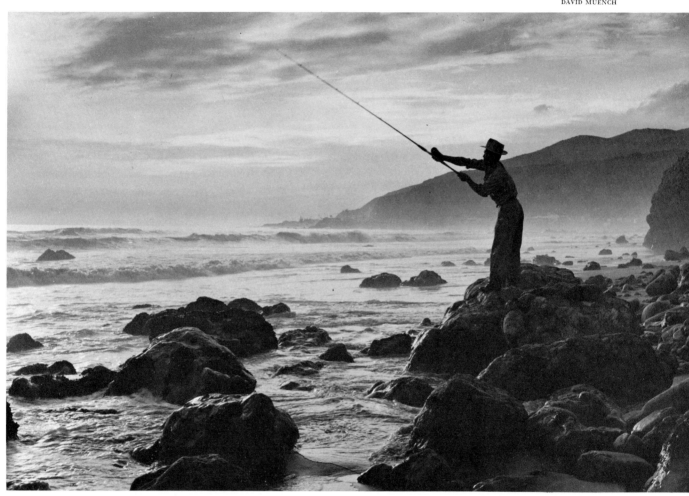

THERE ISN'T MUCH ocean front left for fishermen who favor the surf. Some can find a lonely perch of slippery rock, others band together on a crowded pier. On any Sunday in June, 150 fishermen will drop their lines from the Redondo pier — in the friendly presence of 300 to 400 strolling kibitzers. Either surf or pier, the gunnysacks fill with perch, corvina, spotfin, yellow croakers, and sometimes a small but innocent shark.

GAME FISH MUST BE TRACKED miles out at sea, and the party boats are sturdy ocean-going
vessels that sometimes range as far as Mexican waters, often sailing before dawn. Here, a
party leaves *Long Beach* at midday for a shorter run to the offshore islands, seeking albacore,
barracuda, or yellowtail.

BEACHCOMBERS' HABITAT, the slippery intertidal zone

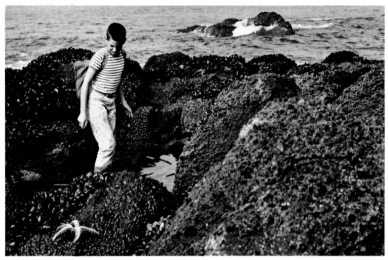

WALTER HOUK

FOR THE AGILE explorer armed with a tide table, the minus tides of February expose innumerable discoveries and curiosities. Bizarre creatures that thrive in a violent environment — tough little animals that survive the pounding of waves that destroy steel ships; adaptable creatures that live in an all-or-nothing world of wet/dry, hot/cool, alternating as the surf ebbs and flows.

RALPH POOLE

RALPH POOLE

A PROWL among the tide pools surely will turn up the familiar sea urchin and anemone (ABOVE), but sometimes something quite unexpected comes in view: (BELOW) a ship's pulley, torn from a wreck by the battering waves, or the imprint of a million-year-old fossil in a sandstone block.

RALPH POOLE

GEORGE WOO

SHIPWRECKS ARE LESS COMMON along this shore than farther north — navigation is simpler and there are fewer marine obstructions — but tragic errors do occur. The battered hulk of the Dominator, lying off Palos Verdes, has been stubbornly resisting the pounding of the waves since 1961 and is now almost gone.

GLENN CHRISTIANSEN

WILLIAM DELORME

PORT WATCHING and other amenities

AN ILLUSION OF ANTIQUITY pervades the simulated century-old California village known as Ports of Call and the New England Whaler's Wharf located in the Ports of Call area at San Pedro . Planned and built from the piling up, the collection of dockside shops and restaurants, with crooked cobbled streets and quaint buildings, stretches along the main channel of the port. Diners in the restaurants have a grandstand view of the motley procession of freighters, ocean liners, kayaks, sloops, harbor patrol boats, and amphibian planes that frequent the channel. A captive ferryboat (Sierra Nevada), *retired from San Francisco Bay, offers shopping and dining facilities. A pleasant place to shop, dine, or stroll, the village is the most extensive and homogeneous of the high-class restaurant and shopping complexes scattered the length of the coast.*

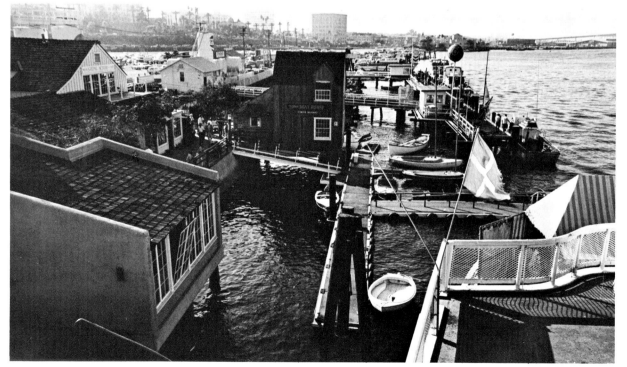

"IN ALL THE WORLD
no trip like this"

*CATALINA ISLAND would not
be the same without the stately
S.S. Catalina, which has been steaming
to and fro since 1928.*

*ONCE A HIDEOUT for buccaneers and smugglers, Catalina Island has been a romantic
destination for pleasure-seekers ever since 1887 when the resort town of Shatto City — shortly
renamed Avalon — was opened and steamer service started with the mainland. The atmosphere
is relaxing, semitropical. Car-less Crescent Drive along the beach is quiet and almost unoccupied
early in the morning, but teems with activity while the boat is in.*

EXHILARATION OF SURF AND SEA **105**

Green Islands in an Urban Sea

A hundred-odd parks, scattered from shoreline to mountain crest; charming remnants of the past, appealing oases of the present; one, the world's largest.

HISTORY IN THE PARK—real and imaginary

CENTURY-OLD WISTERIA vine weighs down arbor at Banning Park, Wilmington, onetime home of an energetic pioneer, General Phineas Banning, typical of a handful of willful men who singlehandedly boosted the growth of Los Angeles. Within a few years after arriving in 1851, Banning, "The Pathfinder," built wharves, founded a city (Wilmington, 1858), planted experimental acres of citrus, set up stage and freight lines, built a railroad from tidewater to downtown Los Angeles (1869), dabbled in lumbering and wagon manufacturing.

THE RIBS OF COVERED WAGONS, a stockade, cannon, and log horses keep youngsters happily warring against each other in Chatsworth Park, a vast rock-strewn oak grove set aside for recreational use by the city of Chatsworth. Other notable city parks that go beyond the customary Civil-War-cannon-on-a-handkerchief-of-grass are in Redlands, Ontario, Pasadena, Beverly Hills. In Long Beach, Bixby Park serves as host for "The World's Largest Picnic," the famous annual reunion of 125,000 nostalgic Iowans.

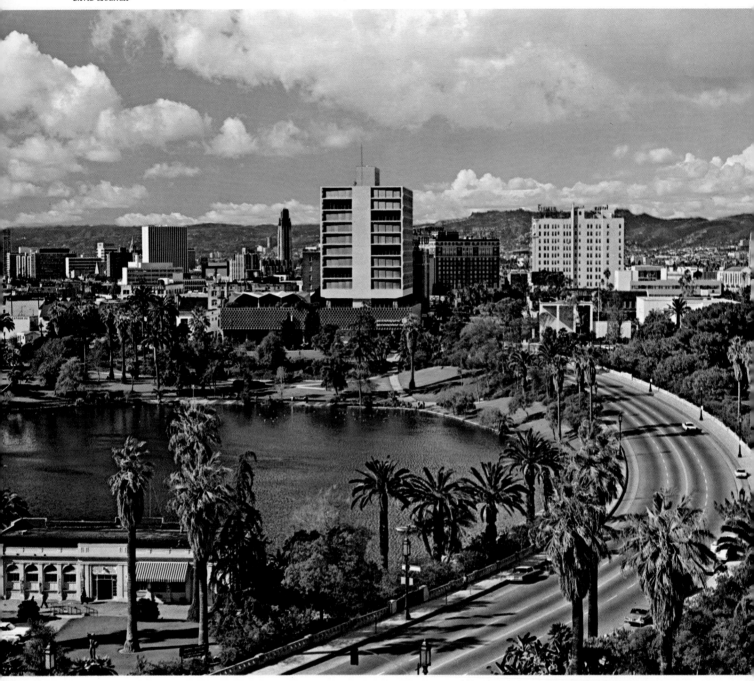

A LOS ANGELES TRADEMARK, MacArthur Park has been a bucolic favorite since it was built from salt marsh in 1890 on what was then the westernmost edge of town. Appropriately christened Westlake, it was renamed for the popular general in 1942. The park is bisected by Wilshire Boulevard, which originally stopped at its border, by a causeway completed in 1941 after years of controversy between rival merchant groups: those to the west sought direct access to downtown, fought with those to the east, who were fearful of losing to Wilshire's blandishments.

MACARTHUR PARK—once country, now urban

A ROLLICKING "Twelfth Night" holds a summer audience spellbound in MacArthur's open-air theater, also used for band concerts and amateur talent shows. Ever a popular park (LEFT), the lake has attracted boatmen, ducks, and pretty girls from the first, as evident in this 1910 period piece.

109

WILLIAM APLIN

BLESSING OF THE ANIMALS brings life back to Plaza Park, one-time center of Los Angeles. On the day before Easter, any pet that can be moved, from a turtle to an ox, can participate in the colorful observance. Some pets are ridden, driven, or led; others are carried in arms, cages, paper bags, or bowls. Many of the people wear Mexican costumes, many of the animals sport garlands of flowers or ribbons. A padre, aided by his altar boys, blesses each animal as it goes by. The custom dates back 1,600 years, has been observed in the Plaza for more than 30 years. At Christmas time, the Plaza echoes to the plaintive songs of "Las Posadas," as candle-bearing pilgrims journey around the square in the traditional Mexican celebration, re-enacting the nine-day search of Mary and Joseph for lodging in Bethlehem.

PLAZA PARK—heart of old Los Angeles

DINIZ '64

PLAZA HISTORICAL Monument, as it may look when it is finally completed, is planned as a mid-19th century restoration closed to traffic except for horse-drawn vehicles. The Pico House (1869) at the right will again become an operating hotel and restaurant — it was once the city's finest — and there will be specialty shops and a theater for melodrama. Already restored: a firehouse and the Masonic temple. Beset by lack of funds, the park has been slow in developing.

BARON WOLMAN

ONE OF THE FEW standing reminders of the Spanish-Mexican origins of the city is the Plaza Church, built in 1814–22, refaced with brick in 1860 when heavy rains nearly washed it away, and recently modernized. Nearby in Olvera Street (page 272) is the city's oldest dwelling, the Avila Adobe, a veritable mansion when built in 1824, now a charming if musty museum.

NOSTALGIA ON WHEELS for
the young in heart at Griffith Park

TO THE SPRIGHTLY
tootling of a calliope,
Griffith's carousel carries on
the fading tradition of the
merry-go-round. The 40-year-
old machine is one of a dozen
carousels still whirling in
the Los Angeles area.

BARRY ANDERSON

THE SMALL BOY IN EVERYONE is brought out by the captive vehicles in Griffith Park's Travel Town, where children and adults may poke, inspect, walk through, and sit in an assortment of retired locomotives, tenders, cabooses, street cars, and other ancient rolling stock.

ENGINEER OF A 1-INCH SCALE 0-4-0 locomotive replenishes water from a scale model water tank in the miniature railroad yard. Tiny steam locomotives pull trainloads of full size passengers around a miniscule track on Sunday afternoons.

GREEN ISLANDS IN AN URBAN SEA   113

WILD ANIMALS go first-cabin in brand new zoo

THE FIRST LARGE ZOO in modern times to be planned and built from scratch, the new Los Angeles Zoo in Griffith Park was opened in 1966 with accommodations for 3,200 animals — and 3,200 cars. Dominated by the twin-towered Zoo Theme Building in its center, the 110-acre compound replaced an installation of 40-years' standing that still is being used as a holding area for new animals and a sanitarium for the ailing. Built on raw ground, the zoo appeared somewhat barren when this photograph was taken before opening day. Many of the trees gracing the compound were transplanted full-grown from the path of freeways.

CURIOUS BEARS AND PEOPLE inspect each other across the protective moat in the North American section, one of the five continental areas where the animals, birds, and plants are grouped to approximate the natural environment. (One of these grizzlies slid down into the moat soon after the zoo was opened and spent a few unhappy days pacing the bottom before she could be enticed back to the company of her fellows.)

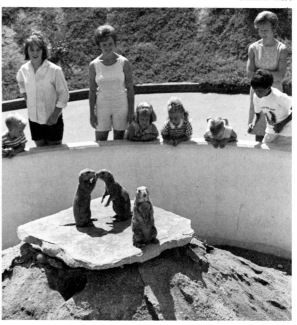

PRAIRIE DOG CLAN goes about its daily activities in the children's zoo, where small animals may be seen close up or met on a person-to-person basis.

GREEN ISLANDS IN AN URBAN SEA **115**

Wilderness at the Doorstep

*A vast mountain sanctuary awaits the city dweller;
pleasuring-ground for the athlete or the nature-lover,
for birders and hunters, and surfers in stretch pants.*

OVER THE MOUNTAINS and through the woods

MARTIN LITTON

*IN THE NEARBY SAN GABRIELS, hikers and horsemen can roam over 433 miles of
trail. In 1962, 136,000 fishermen tried their luck in the stocked streams of Angeles National Forest;
hunters took 850 mule deer, one black bear. In the suburbs, rock-climbers (RIGHT) test
their skills on Stoney Point, Chatsworth, an elementary ascent used by Sierra Clubbers as
qualification for more difficult climbs. On Sundays, the precipice is encrusted with earnest
cliffhangers. The sandstone face is mottled with the names and initials of lovers, sprayed on from
aerosols by the smitten, and periodically erased by civic-minded climbers.*

VICTOR STEIN

MILE-HIGH resort country, backdrop for a hundred movies

SNOW-COVERED ARROWHEAD VILLAGE is a Swiss Christmas card within a three-hour drive of balmy Los Angeles. Although located in the heart of a national forest, the lakes and environs of Arrowhead and neighboring Big Bear are privately owned and intensively developed with homes, cabins, resorts, shops, taverns. The mountainous setting has a familiar look to sharp-eyed devotees of late-late shows on television, for its forests have been a favorite location for motion pictures, standing-in for Alaska, the Rockies, or Canadian wilds in winter, and in summer for the Appalachians, Mohawk country, Black Forest. During the summer months wind-chopped waters of Arrowhead (RIGHT) support an armada of sail and power boats.

LAKE ARROWHEAD DIVISION

UNPREDICTABLE BUT NO STRANGER to the Los Angeles mountains, snow occasionally falls from November to March. Storms are intense while they last but they seldom block the roads, which are kept open through the winter. The white mantle sometimes covers the mountains near Newhall (ABOVE) and bands the flanks of the San Gabriels down to the 2,000-foot contour. The white blanket is visible all over the metropolitan area — a gigantic billboard announcing that there are ski tows running and snowballs to be made Up There. Small resorts, such as mile-high Kratka Ridge (RIGHT) offer refreshments, accommodations, thawing warmth.

CHRISTMAS SURPRISE — snow an hour away from home

121

IN NO OTHER PLACE having an average January temperature of 55° do so many people own winter sports outfits as in the Los Angeles area. A mere hour's drive from the base of the mountains brings snow buffs to any one of a score of ski resorts. Such proximity draws enthusiasts en masse, including a large portion of the surfing crowd in winter plumage; and in the San Gabriels alone, 150,000 skiers will visit the lifts during a good winter. For the summer skier, plastic-covered slopes (RIGHT) duplicate the feel of snow under the skis — but not under the skier, should he have the misfortune to fall.

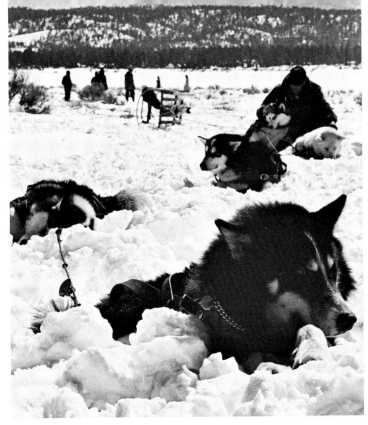

JIM HOLLON

SLED-DOG RACES held annually in Southland mountains add a Klondike fillip to the Angeleno's diversified use of the winter scene. Since 1954, races have been run near Big Bear. In years when there is no snow, dogs pull wheeled sleds.

C. BARRY HAMMONS

The Great Desert Playground

Land of contrasts, the desert is both playground and retreat: a place of stillness and far horizons, of spring wildflowers by the mile—and summer sports in winter.

FROM ONE END of the continent to the other—vertically

PALM SPRINGS AERIAL TRAMWAY

IN ONE GIDDY SWOOP, an aerial tramway covers the equivalent of a trip from Mexico to northern Canada in 15 minutes. Bridging climatic and ecological extremes in its brief ride, the tram connects a wilderness park at the 8,500-foot level in the San Jacintos to Palm Springs in the urbanized desert below. There may be snow at the upper end of the ascent, but at the lower, the mellow winter sun shines on golfers in shirt sleeves.

DESERT WILDFLOWER extravaganza —a link with the past

THE DAZZLING SPRING displays of color that once blanketed the Los Angeles plain have long since disappeared under the metropolitan spread, but a breathtaking taste of how this dramatic sight once appeared can still be enjoyed in the Mojave, an hour or so away. The glowing candelabra of the yucca signal the arrival of spring, but the grand climax comes with the blossoming of vast fields of poppies. Seeing this, it is easy to understand why this bright blossom inspired poets and, earlier, caused Spanish sailors to come ashore to worship the miraculous sight which they had spied from far at sea.

". . . On hills and plains,
Lifting, exultant, every kingly cup
Brewed with the golden vintage of the sun."
Ina Coolbrith, 1905

SAILING on the high desert

LEONARD NADEL

IN SPRING AND FALL when the desert winds are brisk (but not churning the Santa Anas) and suntime temperatures are tolerable, wheeled sports vehicles of all kinds meet on the dry lakes and dunes: motorcycles, dune buggies, and, most picturesque, sand yachts. The latter, pictured here, are handled the same as their waterborne relatives, can zip along at 65 miles an hour. Recently re-introduced in the Los Angeles area, sand sailing is old hat in Europe, where it has been practiced since the early 1600's in Denmark, Belgium, and Holland.

129

Grand-scale Diversions

*For the restless, a rich choice of open-air, all-year
amusements: performing dolphins, waxen movie stars,
race tracks, two ball parks, villages of make-believe.*

OUTDOOR CIRCUS for beasts of the sea

ERNEST BRAUN

*FOUR DOLPHINS LEAP 15 feet through the air in a precision swoop and (RIGHT)
three-quarters of a ton of whale jets out of his tank for a tidbit of food as a part of the sea
animal circus that is repeated three times daily all through the year at Marineland of the
Pacific, Palos Verdes, most extensive and elaborate of the marine parks. In addition to the
acrobatics, Marineland offers a grand mixture of sea creatures that can be viewed close up.
Towering above the compound rises the 315-foot Sky Tower with a rotating glass elevator built in
Switzerland, shipped disassembled on the deck of a vessel. (En route it was mistaken for a
load of missiles by a Navy patrol, which overhauled the ship for red-faced interrogation.)*

TAME DEER, tropical birds, free beer
— two beguiling nature parks

FRATERNIZING WITH DEER is encouraged in Japanese Deer Park, located in Buena Park, where visitors may stroll amid a herd of 200 tame deer and feed and pet the graceful animals from Japan, India, England. Inspired by a famous park in Nara, Japan, the tranquil retreat is graced with a lagoon (ABOVE) and an authentic teahouse.

A DELIGHTFUL TOUR-DE-FORCE of tropical and mountain landscapes linked by waterways, Busch Gardens in San Fernando Valley were three years and four and a half million dollars in the making. Visitors enter by means of a monorail (LEFT) that soars through the Anheuser-Busch brewhouse and deposits them near the gardens, where they may roam about on foot or afloat, take in a bird show or stop for refreshments in one of the pavilions (ABOVE). The 17½-acre gardens are patterned after a similar attraction in Tampa, Florida.

GRAND-SCALE DIVERSIONS   133

HARNESS RACERS SWEEP around half-mile track at the Los Angeles County Fair at Pomona in one of the daily (except Sunday) events of the 12-race card that also features quarter horse and thoroughbred contests. Concentrated in two weeks, the races draw the third highest daily attendance in the state. Part of the income from pari-mutuel wagering (outlawed in California from 1909-1933) is devoted to expenses of operating this, other fairs.

FORTY TONS OF HOT DOGS, 35 tons of hamburger, and a lake of soft drinks are consumed by the million visitors that crowd the fairground for the 17-day festivities. Largest county fair in the nation (487 acres, parking for 45,000 cars), it underwrites an often overlooked fact that urbanized Los Angeles County is still a significant producer of agricultural output (seventh county in the state). Fairgrounds are intensively used throughout the year: Scout-O-Ramas, picnics (5,600 German-Americans), drag strip heats (60,000 fans), shooting meets, horse shows, horse auctions ($3 million worth of horseflesh changes hands), cat show (1,200 fans), pigeon shows (150 attendance), rabbit show (180 fans), coin show (4,000 numismatists).

L.A. CO. FAIR ASSOCIATION

VINTAGE CARS and veteran planes in concourse

PRE-FREEWAY MOTORCARS in all their splendor are on view in Briggs Cunningham Automotive Museum, Costa Mesa. Spanning 55 years, collection includes (LEFT) a 1912 Mercer Raceabout, used by New Jersey police to catch speeders; a 1911 American Underslung with 41-inch wheels; and (BELOW) resplendent Rolls Royces.

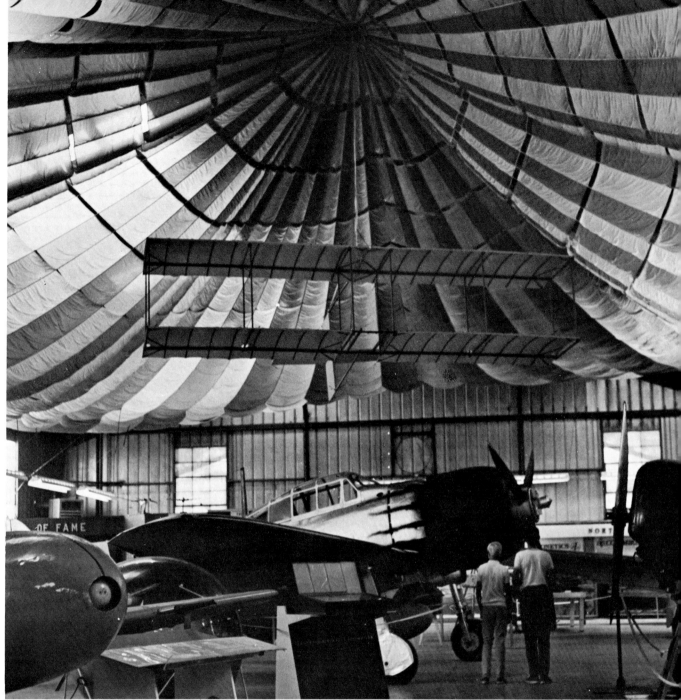

WALTER HOUK

EARLIEST PRODUCTS of the airplane industry are displayed at Orange County Airport and (ABOVE) at the Air Museum at Ontario, which has more than a hundred veteran aircraft — many are still flyable, some are former movie stars. Lofty canopy is Mercury space capsule parachute; from it is suspended an 1895 Chanute glider; on floor, the only Japanese Zero on display in this country. (LEFT): Sun reveals frame inside thin skin of World War I Jenny, oldest (1917) still-flying craft on view. Collection is largest in the West, includes antique craft, pioneering jets, and veterans of World War II, including several German examples.

WALTER HOUK

THE HAPPIEST PLACE in the world—
Walt Disney's 65-acre stage where every
visitor is an actor

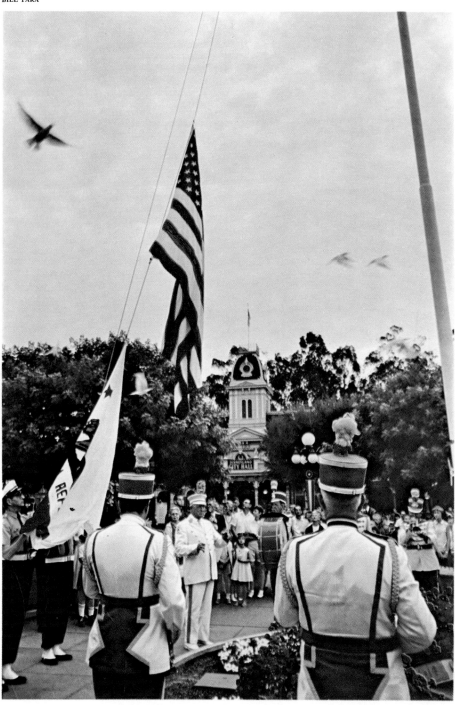

*THERE IS A DISARMING quality
about Disneyland that dissolves even
the most cynical into wholesome
camaraderie. A natural offshoot of
the motion picture industry, the
enterprise relies on the imagination
and cunning of set designers to
transport visitors backward and
forward in time, subject them
safely to situations of direst
peril, and surround them with
happy sights and sounds. The
magnitude of the illusion is typical
of the grand-scale ways of
Los Angeles, for Disneyland is
one of the largest (65 acres), best
attended (6.4 million a year) of
the world's amusement parks.
Nightly ceremony (LEFT) of striking
the colors is accompanied by tootling
of the national anthem; (RIGHT)
throughout the summer, fireworks
sprout from the castle several times
a week.*

AUTOMOBILITY AND GOOD FOOD have combined to elevate a roadside stand in a berry patch, located miles from nowhere in 1920, to an extraordinary recreational complex that draws patrons from all over the Los Angeles area. Family-run Knott's Berry Farm and Ghost Town, Buena Park, covers 200 acres (50 for parking) with 42 gift shops, seven restaurants, and a ghost town (BELOW) complete with gold mine, 1880 railroad imported from Colorado, a gold-panning stream. Also on the grounds stands a brick-by-brick duplicate of Independence Hall, erected by the patriotic proprietors as a tribute to the ideals of the Founding Fathers.

IMMORTALIZED IN WAX, Laurel and Hardy sit cheerfully amid the shards of a Model T in a set at Movieland Wax Museum, Buena Park, established as a "living history of the glamorous people and memorable films of Hollywood." A hundred actors are shown in 60 sets, frozen in climactic scenes from their best-known films. This museum is the only one in the area devoted exclusively to the history of the movie industry.

KNOTT'S BERRY FARM

REAL AND UNREAL blend in the coffee shop where patrons share the tables with wax film dummies.

GRAND-SCALE DIVERSIONS   141

HORSE RACING FEVER,
contagious since Spanish days

RAIN OR SHINE, horses race through the winter at Santa Anita — and bettors race for their favorite, "lucky" seats (ABOVE). Santa Anita is near the site of a pioneer track developed by Lucky Baldwin, colorful millionaire and breeder of champion racers (1880–90). Introduced by the Spaniards in late 1700's, horse races were run near the missions during fiestas. By the 1860's, racing was featured in a dozen county fairs and, by early 1900's, breeding of race horses had become the state's third largest industry. Racing and horse breeding declined after wagering was outlawed in 1909, only to revive in 1933 when the sport was legalized under state supervision. Two tracks in Los Angeles County — Santa Anita (opened in 1934) and Hollywood Park (1938) — together account for more than half the state's income from pari-mutuel taxes, even though they draw less than a fifth of the racing fans.

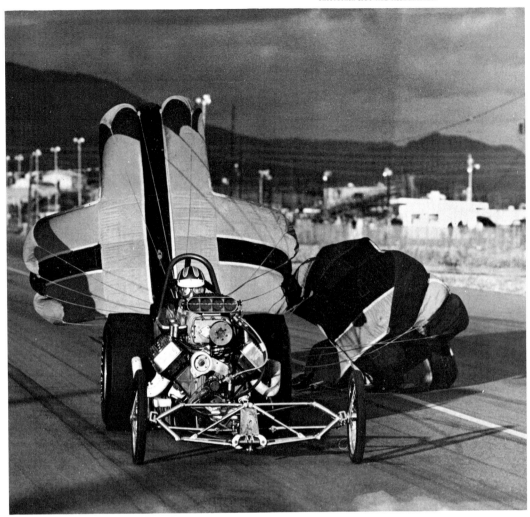

*TRAILING PARACHUTES,
dragster slows to a halt
after sprint at the County
Fairgrounds in Pomona.
Native to Los Angeles,
vehicles originated here in
1950's, first dragstrip in
country opened at Santa Ana
Airport in 1952. Key to drag
racing is tremendous
acceleration from standing
start over straight quarter-mile
course. Champion drivers
have covered course in less
than eight seconds, reached
over 200 miles an hour.
Timing is by electronic
devices, times are in
milliseconds.*

FOR MOTORMANIACS—big-time speed classics

DUELING FOR POSITION on the Riverside Raceway, three racing Porsches and a
*Lotus Ford (98) round a U-turn in the Los Angeles Times Grand Prix, an annual (since 1957)
classic that attracts racers from around the world to compete for its generous purses. The
Raceway, an h-shaped, 3.2-mile paved track, is the setting for five major racing events that
draw 275,000 fans a year. Car racing has been popular in the area since the 1910's,
when a series of road and track races brought national renown.*

L.A. TIMES

MAJOR LEAGUE baseball doubleheader

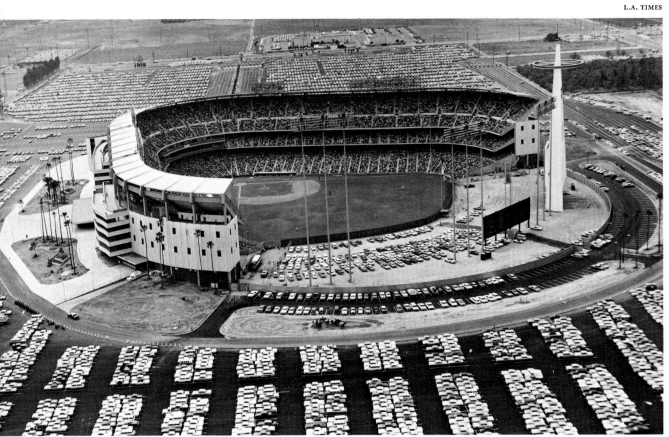

CALIFORNIA ANGELS *play here. Modern stadium (1967) in Anaheim is home base for the second big league ball club to set up shop in the area. Home-owned, home-grown, the American League team is named nostalgically for a minor league club that represented Los Angeles in the Pacific Coast League from 1903–1957. Stadium seats 43,204 fans with potential capacity of 50,000; parking for 12,000 cars and 200 buses; total compound, 140 acres.*

UNIFORMS *for the two Los Angeles area teams that rarely meet (they belong to different leagues). Feature of Angels' uniform: a halo around the rim of the cap. Between them, the two clubs draw a quarter of the area's expenditures on spectator sports.*

LOS ANGELES DODGERS play here. First major league team in Los Angeles, the 69-year-old club moved West from Brooklyn in 1958 and following year took possession of huge new stadium built for them near Chavez Ravine. National League pennant winners, the club brought to Los Angeles the first World Series played west of the Mississippi River. Since coming here, the team has broken all-time attendance records (2,750,000 in 1962). Largest turnout is usually for games with old rivals, San Francisco Giants, also expatriates from New York.

GRAND-SCALE DIVERSIONS 147

ROSE BOWL, granddaddy of the intersectionals

SWARMING AROUND THE STATUE of Tommy Trojan, USC students give the victory sign as they whoop it up over the news that their football team has been chosen to play in the Rose Bowl. Both USC and UCLA receive unabashed support for their outstanding athletic programs and both have represented the Pacific Athletic Conference many times in the Rose Bowl.

IT SHOULD READ "WASHINGTON"! In one of the noblest college pranks of all time, Caltech students subverted the half-time card stunts of the Washington-Minnesota game of 1961 causing an astonished rooting section to flash CALTECH instead of WASHINGTON before a national television audience. The detailed hoax was a flowering of Caltech's tradition of undergraduate tomfoolery.

SINCE 1902, football teams from major western and eastern colleges have fought it out in Pasadena's annual New Year's classic. Under sunny skies (46 out of 53 days), the West has won 22, lost 28, and tied 3 games.

Festivals Herald the Seasons

Many are the ways for a community to salute the calendar:
celebrate roses in winter or the summer harvest of fish,
stage Oriental pageantry, proclaim a festival of fine arts.

WINTER FLOWER FETE that became a national tradition

MARTIN LITTON

FINISHING TOUCHES on a Tournament of Roses float involve feverish activity. The thousands
of fresh (NO artificial) blossoms that cover a float arrive from growing grounds in
California, Florida, and Hawaii a day or two before and are attached individually by hand
on New Year's Eve. The most sought-after decorators are students of religious oriented
colleges who are immune to the temptations of New Year's revelry. Girls who ride the floats
must be on hand hours before the parade, sometimes catnap among the chrysanthemums.
Spectators camp by the thousands along the parade route the night before.

ELABORATE OUTGROWTH *of a village flower fete and sports tourney staged in 1890, the parade of 60 floats moves sedately down Pasadena's Colorado Boulevard in a 3-hour show seen by 70 million television viewers across the country. The floats are made of a mass of chickenwire and steel, covered with a cocoon of sprayed plastic to hold the flowers. Some floats are modified and re-used in Portland Rose Festival, New Orleans' Mardi Gras. Designing and fabricating floats is full-time business for a half dozen firms in the area.*

151

JAPAN IN LOS ANGELES—summer is festival time

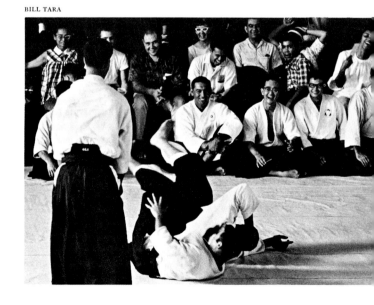

CLIMAX IN A SERIES of summer festivals in Little Tokyo, Nisei Week (founded 1934) is an elaborate celebration of Japanese traditions that culminates in the captivating ondo *parade (ABOVE). The week is crowded with demonstrations of manly sports (RIGHT) and the gentler arts of flower arranging, calligraphy, and the tea ceremony. Great care is lavished on the rich costumes (LEFT), which represent different regions of Japan. Girls start preparing weeks ahead for the parade, sewing costumes and perfecting the intricate rhythms of the* ondo *dances. Although the largest population of Japanese on the mainland lives in Los Angeles, few reside in Little Tokyo proper (First Street between Los Angeles and Central), which remains a cultural and commercial center. Japanese first settled here in the 1880's as farmers, fishermen, and later as landscape gardeners. By 1941, 30,000 lived in the neighborhood of the Civic Center; but they were brusquely dispersed during World War II, and when they returned later, they settled throughout the region.*

COLORFUL PENNANTS FLY by the hundreds from decorated fishing boats lined up in
Los Angeles Harbor for the annual Fishermen's Fiesta, held in September or October, depending
on the catch. A combination of carnival and religious rite, the fiesta fills a weekend with boat
rides, contests in net-mending, rope-tying and splicing, native dances by members of the national
groups living in San Pedro, and it culminates with the grand water parade down the main channel.
Boat decorations are elaborately conceived, many are animated.

FISHERMEN'S FIESTA to celebrate the sea's bounty

BARON WOLMAN

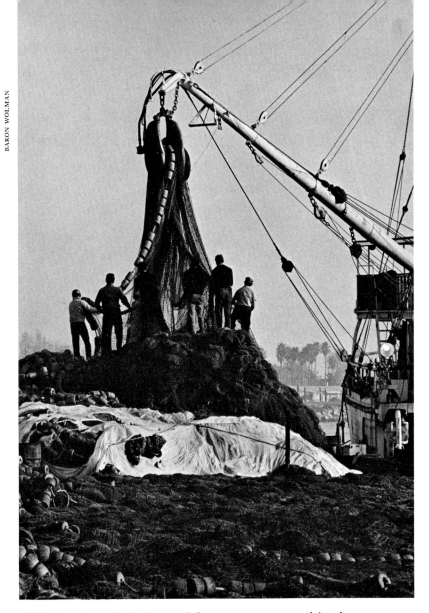

FISHERMEN INSPECT one of the enormous nets used for deep sea fishing. Technological advances in fish-catching gear keep pressure on popular fish species to the point of extinction. Fish have to contend with powered net pullers, depth finders, scouting planes, radiotelephones, sonar, lighted lures, and mile-long nets. Some boats are virtual floating factories.

WILLIAM APLIN

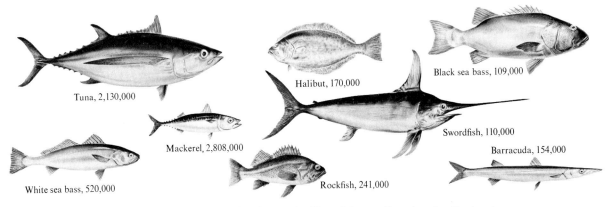

Tuna, 2,130,000

Halibut, 170,000

Black sea bass, 109,000

Mackerel, 2,808,000

Swordfish, 110,000

Barracuda, 154,000

White sea bass, 520,000

Rockfish, 241,000

LEADING FISHING PORT in volume and value in the United States, Los Angeles Harbor is also the center of the nation's largest seafood canning industry. Principal catch is made up of the commercial fish portrayed above, with 1965 poundage indicated for each fish. Not shown: anchovies, 158,000; sardine, 339,000; kingfish, 388,000 pounds.

155

ARTS FESTIVAL and pageant of the Old Masters

VISITORS STROLL THROUGH the outdoor art show held each year in Laguna Beach by the art association for its annual Festival of the Arts and Pageant of the Masters. Limited to artists living in the immediate area, the show displays about 200 selected pieces. One of the oldest art shows in the state, it goes back to 1913 when the first members of the art colony hung their paintings on fences. A permanent gallery was built in 1918, replaced in 1928, enlarged in 1952. Artists discovered Laguna Beach in the 1890's when it was remote and inaccessible. First-comers camped on the bluffs and recorded the unspoiled grandeur on canvas. In time, summer houses appeared, followed by permanent residences, and Laguna was on its way to becoming a city for creative artists.

LAGUNA FESTIVAL OF ART

MODELS STAND STOCK-STILL
as Mexican chessmen in a classic
checkmate position on the stage of the
Pageant of the Masters in Laguna Beach.
Since 1932, crowds have gathered here
to see famous paintings and classic
sculptures re-created by living models,
in a community effort that utilizes a
voluntary cast of 600. The show closes
traditionally with Da Vinci's Last Supper,
here being checked out (RIGHT) *by the*
producer. The pageant was launched in the
depths of the Depression as an act of
desperation by the art colony, starving for
lack of customers. It now attracts
250,000 spectators a year.

157

Ferment in the Performing Arts

Classics under the stars, Shakespeare in the park, fine music and drama in converted stores, museums, and marble palaces—the choices are rich and wide.

RARE MUSICAL FARE on the campus and in the museums

RICHARD FISH

ELECTRIFYING MUSIC of gamelan *instruments accompanies costumed Indonesian dancer at the International Festival of Music and Dance held annually at UCLA by its Institute of Ethnomusicology. The Institute draws on its large collection of musical instruments and costumes from many lands to help stage the shows effectively. This series is just one of the many unusual events on local campuses that provide a rich supplement to the concert season.*

*IN A SUNDAY AFTERNOON CONCERT at the Los Angeles County Museum of Natural
History, members of the Wakita Koto Chamber Ensemble perform Japanese music (ABOVE)
on the koto (Japanese harp) and bamboo flute, and (BELOW) performers with the Elizabeth Waldo
Folkloric Group specializing in Indian music play a pre-Columbian ceramic flute
and an Apache Indian one-string violin. Concerts of ethnic music supplement the usual fare of
classical chamber music that has been given here continuously for seventeen years and broadcast
to an audience of 400,000 music lovers. Another distinguished chamber series, held in the
County Museum of Art, has been making musical history for twenty-five years
as the Monday Evening Concerts, a subscription series devoted uncompromisingly to
works of contemporary composers.*

FERMENT IN THE PERFORMING ARTS   **159**

SUMMER EVENING symphony
under a starlit sky

*AS EASTER DAWN BREAKS over the Hollywood
Hills, a swelling chorus of song heralds the joyful event
from the shell of the Hollywood Bowl in a memorable
celebration that has drawn thousands of the devout
since 1921. The famous Bowl is equally well-known for
its "Symphonies Under the Stars," a summer series that
attracts the romantically inclined to bask in classical
music played in the balmy open air. What was once a
simple bandstand in the center of a weedy dell is now
a complex amphitheater that accommodates 20,000 in
one sitting, 300,000 in a summer.*

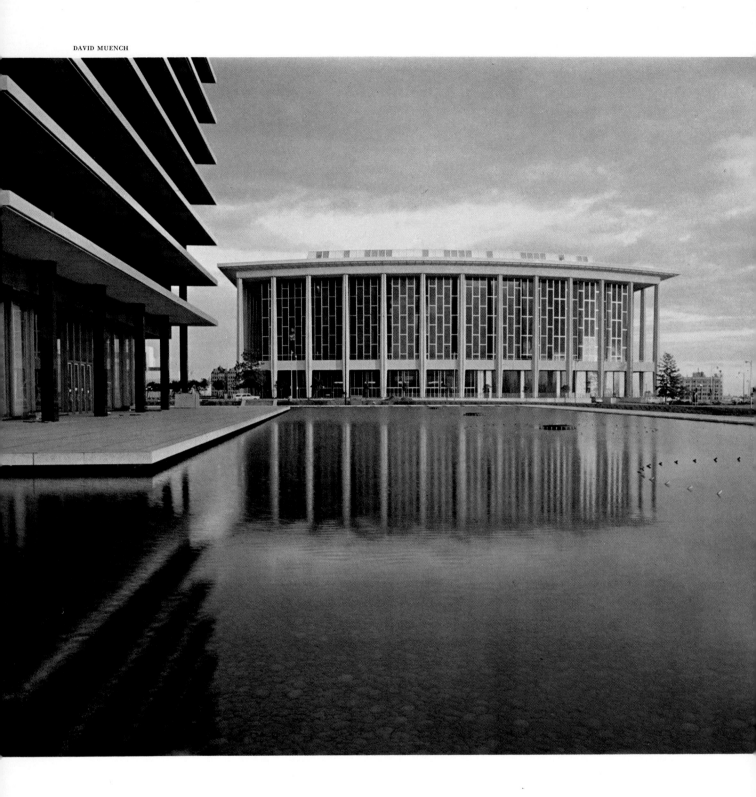

AN ELEGANT MONUMENT to cultural enterprise

IN A SETTING of quiet splendor and tranquil beauty, the elegant Dorothy Chandler Pavilion stands as a monument to the success of a coalition of government and private enterprise that probably is unique to Los Angeles. Of the $34 million that it cost, half was provided by the County and half by individual donors, inspired by the indefatigable civic leader for whom the Pavilion is named. The marble and black glass music hall is the home of the Philharmonic Orchestra, a prestigious fixture of the musical scene since 1919. The Pavilion (completed in 1964) was the first in the Music Center complex of three theaters, linked on the surface by a landscaped mall and underground by a vast parking cavern.

DOROTHY CHANDLER PAVILION

HOWARD AHMANSON THEATRE

MARK TAPER FORUM

WELTON BECKET & ASSOCIATES

MAURICE E. MANSON

ADVANCED CONCEPTS in theatrical design are incorporated in the Pavilion. A movable acoustical shell of gilded fiberglass, which carries the pure sound of the music to the farthest seat, can be set for symphony, opera, or musical comedy. Seating on the auditorium floor is continental style with no center aisle. A profusion of exits permits the 1,500 patrons on the lower floor to leave quickly and easily — in a minute and a half, if need be.

FIRST RECORDING made in the Pavilion was by the Los Angeles Philharmonic under the baton of its dynamic conductor, Zubin Mehta, pictured on the jacket.

PEOPLE PROVIDE THE COLOR in the Grand Hall as they cascade down the Grand Stairway, reflected and re-reflected in the mirrored, four-story wall.

165

THEATER OF INNOVATION and experiment, the 750-seat Mark Taper Forum in the Music Center is deceptively simple in design. A hexagonal stage, projecting into the half-round seating, is backed up by an elaborate complex of lights, projectors and screens that enables the producer to surround the actors with settings that are both convincing and imaginative. Committed to drama that is cerebral, demanding, and abrasive, the Forum is operated by a residence company under the Center Theater Group, lured downtown from UCLA where it had performed successfully for eight years. Also used for lectures, chamber music concerts, and intimate opera, the building is linked (RIGHT) to its larger companion, the Ahmanson Theatre, by a lofty colonnade that echoes the design of the Chandler Pavilion across the court.

ON STAGE with a lively repertory

MAURICE F. MANSON

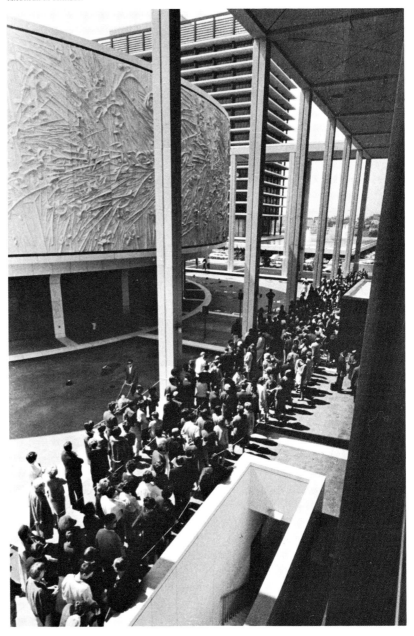

*THEATER-GOERS QUEUE UP for tickets to the dedicatory
performances at the Ahmanson Theatre in 1967, a stark musical version
of "Don Quixote". The spacious, 2,100-seat auditorium completes the
triple complex in the Music Center which collectively offers a concentration
of theatrical fare unique to the West. Dedicated to bringing first-class
plays and musical dramas that have a wider appeal than the experiments
in the Forum, it is operated three-fourths of the year (September–April)
by the Center Theater Group and the rest of the time by the
Los Angeles Civic Light Opera.*

WILTON BECKET & ASSOCIATES

VITAL THEATER in a sumptuous setting

AN IMAGINATIVE PERFORMANCE of Tolstoi's "War and Peace"
(shown on stage above and in rehearsal at right) brought the proficient
APA Repertory to the Greek Theater in Griffith Park for outdoor
performances in 1966. Not an ideal setting for subtle drama, the open-air
theater built in 1930 is ordinarily taken over in summer by more forceful
fare: musical comedy, ballet, jazz bands. The APA, one of the nation's
stellar repertory companies, splits its seasons between New York and
Los Angeles, spends its summers here in the Huntington Hartford Theater,
which it shares with a talented resident group and other visiting
repertories. Supplementing the offerings of this theater are half a hundred
little theaters of widely varying quality scattered over the region and
stocked with actors from the boundless pool of Hollywood talent.

TWO PLAYHOUSES with all-time record runs

PASADENA PLAYHOUSE, a vigorous theater and school of the dramatic arts, may well hold the all-time record for continuous performance. Started in 1916, moved to its present quarters in 1925, expanded in 1936, it probably has produced within its Spanish colonial walls most known plays of significance. Named the State Theater by the Legislature in 1937, it has offered several world premieres and drama festivals, graduated a number of prominent movie stars. Present program features well-known stars in lead roles.

FIFTY YEARS of playbills (1917–1967) symbolize the long career of the Playhouse that has weathered two world wars, influenza epidemics, the coming of radio, the talkies, television, and periodic financial cliffhangers.

PADUA HILLS THEATER, founded in 1932 on a wooded hilltop behind Claremont, has survived through the decades by virtue of the beguiling nature of its blend of theater, restaurant, and handcraft shops. The Mexican fare, both on stage and on the table, is authentic and thoughtfully prepared. The troupe produces original plays, often in Spanish, written around Mexican life, and calls in members of the Mexican colony to help with the dances and plays.

171

Windows on Understanding

Push-button mathematics, death in a tarpit, ancient man and hairy mammoths, constellations on order—such are the wonders of science and nature unveiled in the museums.

INDIAN ARTS on display—from Aztec to Blackfoot

BLACKFOOT INDIAN TEPEE, surrounded by typical weapons, tools, and implements used by Great Plains Indians is a major display in Southwest Museum (founded in 1903), one of the nation's finest collections of southwestern Indian artifacts. Memorable exhibit: relics found under ancient lake bed near Las Vegas, carbon-dated 28,000 years back, place man in same era as the ground sloth.

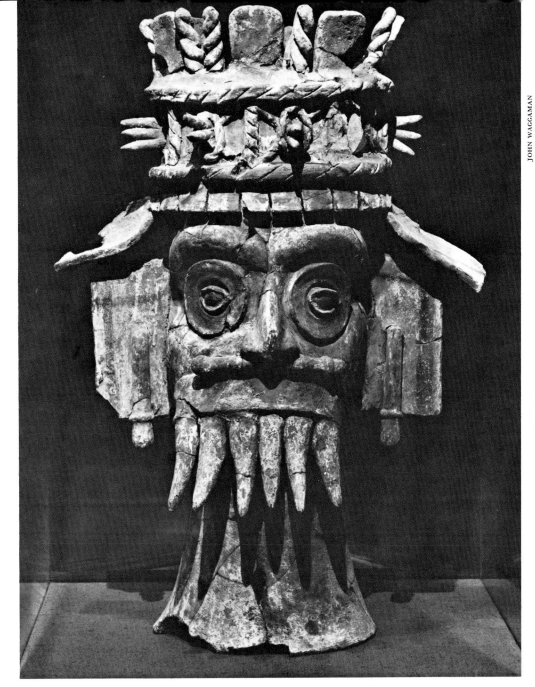

*FIERCE GOD for a fierce
people, rain god of the Aztecs
(1367–1521) of Mexico could
cause snow, hail, rain,
thunder; control rivers and
lakes; cause dropsy, gout, or
rheumatism. Incense burner,
39 inches tall, is one of rare
group of objects from ancient
Latin American civilizations
loaned to Los Angeles County
Museum of Natural History
by public-spirited collectors.*

*DROLL GROUP celebrating
a wedding in a Western
Mexican village (220 BC to
400 AD) is one of several
charming miniatures (this one:
7 inches high) representing
village events (funerals,
religious rites, battles) in
Museum's collection. Display
of ancient art from Latin
America is appropriate to city
with such a large Mexican-
American population.*

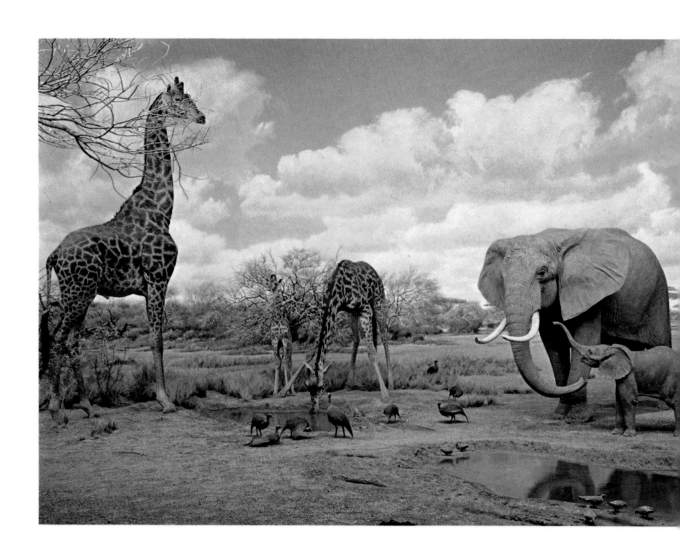

AFRICAN WATERHOLE brought from Kenya to Exposition Park

MAURICE E. MANSON

IT IS EARLY MORNING at the end of the dry season in Kenya and a family of elephants gathers around a water hole. The patriarch stands restlessly, his ears flared to pick up sounds of danger. Not long ago, these majestic animals roamed the African plains until they were brought down by an expedition from the Natural History Museum sent to gather specimens for this vast diorama. The only exhibit of its kind in the world, it conveys an eerie illusion of reality, owing largely to the convincing 116-foot backdrop painted by a skilled scene painter from the motion picture studios. Installation of the exhibit in 1965 (RIGHT) had its clumsy moments. The specimens, formed of fiberglass covered with hide, were shipped to the museum disassembled and had to be pieced together by the staff.

AN AWESOME retrospective at the Natural History Museum

JOHN WAGGAMAN

HUGE SKELETON *of a mammoth, remote ancestor of the elephant, is one of thousands of skeletons exhumed from a tarry grave at La Brea where they had lain for 10,000 to 40,000 years. The collection of bones taken from the pits is the largest in the world, a veritable paleontological bonanza. The mammoth may also be seen fully clothed in a skin of fiberglass at Hancock Park.*

FIRST DENIZENS
of Los Angeles Basin

Mammoth   *La Brea Stork*

BATTLING DINOSAURS fight it out in the rotunda of the museum. The 135-million-year-old skeletons were assembled from bones discovered in Utah. Dinosaurs are not native Angelenos.

Western Horse

Ground Sloth

Mastodon

REVELATIONS of scientific truth at the touch of a button

CHARLES EAMES

BY TURNING KNOBS and pressing buttons in a stunning array of do-it-yourself exhibits in the California Museum of Science and Industry in Exposition Park, visitors can give themselves a short course in basic science. Most notable are the exhibits designed to stimulate interest in mathematics and the physical sciences, such as the IBM display featured on these pages. Understandably popular in a region that is heavily committed to space technology, the museum is patronized by two million visitors a year, thousands of them in classroom lots.

A PINBALL MACHINE in a sophisticated version reveals the laws of orbiting bodies.
Elsewhere in the museum, mathematical principles are demonstrated by ingenious machines
that flash lights and ring bells, use soap bubbles, rubber balls. With simple controls, a child can
manipulate airfoils, change orbits with gravity, fire up a jet engine, turn a car wheel or axle,
or play tic-tac-toe with an electronic brain that never loses.

A MOVING ARROW zips around
a twisted, endless belt known as
Moebius band, a curious form that
has surface but only one side and
one edge, to illustrate a principle in
the branch of mathematics known
as topology.

CONSTELLATIONS-to-order at Griffith Observatory

MAURICE E. MANSON

BUSLOAD OF STUDENTS waits beside an equatorial sundial (accurate to one minute) for a turn to enter the observatory and planetarium in Griffith Park, a mandatory stop for science classes. Opened in 1935 as a bequest of Colonel Griffith J. Griffith, the observatory is crammed with vintage exhibits on astronomy and the physical sciences.

MAURICE E. MANSON

STARS RECEDE and a cloudy sunrise ends the show in the planetarium, projected from an ungainly instrument against a blackened dome. One of the few in the country, the planetarium can duplicate the heavens at any hour, any year. Shows take audiences to the moon and back, around planets; reproduce comets and meteorites, eclipses and auroras; bring back the Star of Bethlehem.

HYPNOTIC SWING of a Foucault pendulum demonstrates rotation of the earth. Pendulum sweeps back and forth on a fixed course while the earth beneath it slowly turns. In a half-hour of bug-eyed watching, the observer can see a noticeable shift of the earth beneath the path of the ball.

WINDOWS ON UNDERSTANDING

CELESTIAL DRAMA
on top of Mount Wilson

GIANT TELESCOPIC CAMERA, the 100-inch, 100-ton Hooker telescope is the largest of the battery of astronomical instruments on top of Mount Wilson, operated by the Carnegie Institute of Washington. Installed in 1918, it has participated in major discoveries, such as recording in 1936 the explosion of a star that disintegrated seven million years ago, and now is scanning the galaxies for clues to the riddles of the space age. (It is open to the public on a limited basis.)

THE SPIRAL NEBULAE AND "GUNSMOKE" share the summit of Mount Wilson, which is occupied by the renowned astronomical observatory and a forest of television transmitters, purveyors to an audience of seven million viewers. It was chosen as an observatory site in 1903 because it was "free of atmospheric disturbance" and was rediscovered a half century later by television engineers seeking a vantage point to reach a vast area. Long before either scientist or engineer discovered the peak, legions of hikers, nature lovers, and tourists had climbed to the top to enjoy the bracing air and to marvel at the 100-mile panoramas.

Showcase for Art Treasures

Lately blossomed as a major art center, Los Angeles enshrines the very old and the very new in marble pavilions and a multitude of galleries.

THE LIVELY art market, professional and amateur

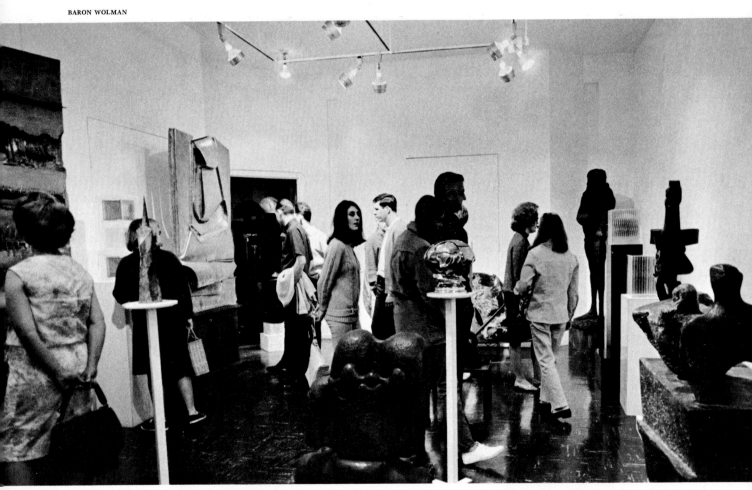

MONDAY EVENING PROMENADE down gallery row along La Cienega Boulevard keeps art fanciers in touch with the latest offerings in a score of galleries that help sustain the area's reputation as a major art market. The strollers roam in and out of open galleries or scan the windows of appointment-only shops, encountering a wide spectrum of taste, ranging from decorator's art to avant garde. Part of the charm of the weekly rite is keeping score on the galleries themselves, which come and go, change owners, names or collections as fortunes shift in a volatile market.

SOME 3,000 PAINTINGS, drawings, sculptures, and other original works are displayed every summer in the mammoth All City Outdoor Art Festival held in Elysian Park. As entries are limited one to an artist and all work submitted is displayed, the show spans an exuberant range of visual experience. Attendance of 60,000 is customary.

PROUD SHOWCASE
for the history of art

THE PALATIAL *Los Angeles County Art Museum, largest built in America since the National Gallery went up in Washington in 1941, is stunning evidence of the region's significance as an art center. In addition to its own extensive holdings, the museum displays priceless private collections, loaned by wealthy art patrons concentrated in the area. As with the Music Center, the museum was funded jointly by government and private contributions, the art patrons underwriting 60 per cent of the $20 million cost. (*BELOW*): Constantly slapped and stirred by jets of water, Alexander Calder's pleasing mobile* Hello Girls *greets museum visitors passing on the plaza.*

PAUL C. JOHNSON

THREE-BUILDING complex is built around a pool-encircled grand entry. Ahmanson Gallery contains the permanent collections. Changing displays are shown in the Special Exhibitions Gallery. Leo S. Bing Center houses a theater, restaurant, art rental and children's galleries. Upper-level court is used for sculpture display. Entire structure rides on a 3-foot-thick concrete raft, floating on the tarpits of La Brea, death trap for antediluvian animals.

AHMANSON GALLERY

L.A. CO. MUSEUM OF ART

SPECIAL EXHIBITIONS GALLERY

LEO S. BING CENTER

WILSHIRE BOULEVARD

187

LUXURY SETTING for a wealth of rare treasures

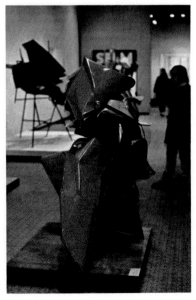

SPANNING THE HISTORY of art, the collections in the Los Angeles County Museum of Art range from ancient treasures, displayed in the Ahmanson on the first level of the lofty atrium court (RIGHT) and the Mosher Gothiç Gallery (ABOVE), to day-after-tomorrow art, shown on the third level (LEFT). Electronic wizardry pampers and protects the priceless art: closed-circuit television "patrols" the galleries, sensors sniff out the faintest wisp of smoke, and air conditioning regulates temperature and humidity, filters out smog, destroyer of paintings and old glass (filters are shipped east for purification). The elaborately equipped buildings were designed by William L. Pereira & Associates.

188

HUNTINGTON GALLERY, an extraordinary public bequest

GALLERY GOERS pause before Gainsborough's
The Blue Boy, *most publicized painting in the Henry E.
Huntington Art Gallery, San Marino. Purchased in 1922
for $620,000, the portrait is merely one masterpiece
in a distinguished ensemble of 18th-century British art,
acknowledged as the best in the country. Prototype of
Los Angeles art collectors and benefactors, Huntington
(1850–1927) was a real estate promoter, head of the
giant Pacific Electric railway net, and a man who "spent
millions with his right hand, pinched pennies with his
left." His collections are housed in a Georgian mansion
(LEFT), bequeathed to the public along with a 200-acre
garden and a priceless library containing a Gutenberg
Bible and original Shakespeare quartos.*

CHELSEA PORCELAIN from the "Gold Anchor" period (1758–1770).

WATTS TOWERS—a heartfelt tribute to beauty

ONE OF THE GENUINE marvels of this century, Rodia's towers in Watts stand as a symbol of creative energy and a shrine for artists. As a supreme example of the arts of assemblage and walk-through sculpture, they are an inspiration to local artists who have made the area known for leadership in these media. The lacy structure of reinforced concrete, richly adorned with bits of tile, broken glass, seashells, and pottery shards, was created over a span of 33 years by an untutored genius, Sabatino Rodia (also known as Simon or Sam Rodia). An immigrant from Italy, he wanted "to do something for the United States because there are nice people in this country." His astonishing tribute is internationally appreciated as a great work of folk art, has been designated by the city as an historic monument, and in time will become the nucleus of a cultural center.

CAMPUS ART
collection par excellence

OUTSTANDING AMONG campus collections in the area (or anywhere, for that matter) is the wealth of art displayed at UCLA in three galleries and a four-and-a-half-acre outdoor sculpture court. Two dozen pieces of 20th century sculpture include works by Henry Moore, Matisse, Archipenko, Laurens, Rodin, and the convoluted Song of the Vowels *by Lipchitz (*RIGHT*) in front of the Dickson Art Center. Inside the center there also are galleries for traveling exhibits and a print room. The Congolese ceremonial mask (*BELOW*) is one of the primitive masterpieces in the nearby Museum and Laboratories of Ethnic Arts and Technology.*

MUSEUM & LABORATORIES
OF ETHNIC ARTS & TECHNOLOGY

BARON WOLMAN

CERAMICS AND TEXTILES, work of graduate art students, is displayed at the end of the semester in the Dickson Art Center. Notable collections on other campuses: portraits and landscapes at USC's Fisher Gallery, murals at Claremont, contemporary sculpture at Long Beach State (see page 220).

ERNEST BRAUN

SHOWCASE FOR ART TREASURES **195**

COMMUNITY INVOLVEMENT in a dynamic, modern museum

AMONG PROUDEST POSSESSIONS of the Pasadena Art Museum are works of the Blue Four, a group of painters formed in Germany in 1924 who strongly influenced the course of modern art. Left to right: Lyonel Feininger, Paul Klee, Wassilj Kandinsky, Alexei von Jawlensky. The museum has the most important ensemble of Klee's works outside of New York.

BARON WOLMAN

ART WORKSHOPS are a dynamic specialty, part of a program to involve the community in the excitement of visual invention and personal participation in the arts. Classes in music, dance, and art often are combined in one. Young dancers interpret rhythms of abstract paintings or, in typical exercise (RIGHT), the chance contours of ribbons cast on the floor.

BARON WOLMAN

Designs for Living

Ways to make the most of climate and terrain; classics in home design, high-rise on the skyline, pools under foot; and an explosion of grace notes from the designers of small things.

PROTOTYPE of the California bungalow

AMBER AND GREEN *stained glass welcome the visitor to the Gamble House (1908), architectural classic in Pasadena, open to the public as a showpiece.*

ERNEST BRAUN

ERNEST BRAUN

ONE OF THE GREAT HOUSES *of two innovating brothers, architects Charles and Henry Greene, stands in Pasadena (4 Westmoreland Place) as a monument to this pair who developed an architecture so original and well adapted to the locale that it spread throughout California — and beyond — as the California bungalow style. Special features that influenced later architecture: climate control by wide roof overhangs, possibilities of indoor-outdoor living on large terraces and roofed decks, integration of garden and house design.*

ERNEST BRAUN

SENSITIVE USE of wood, combined with design influences from the Pacific gives exquisite character to detailing. All exposed surfaces were carefully shaped, finished, decorated. Metal straps, wedges, and pegs that hold house together are integral part of house design.

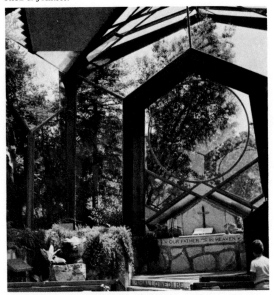

WAYFARERS' CHAPEL, high above Portuguese Bend on the Palos Verdes peninsula, is the creation of Lloyd Wright, famous son of the famous architect. Internationally acclaimed for its design, the church is an imaginative assemblage of glass, laminated redwood and stone, which features the repetition of strong geometric forms: the triangle (symbol of the Holy Trinity) and the circle (symbol of the totality of God). Opened in 1949, it was commissioned by the Church of New Jerusalem as a place of meditation and worship for all faiths.

CREATIVE ARCHITECTURE by the Wrights, father and son

SCORCHINGLY CRITICAL of the "rag-tag" architecture of Southern California, Frank Lloyd Wright nevertheless designed seven houses (1917–39) and an art gallery (1956) for Los Angeles clients. Best of these are Hollyhock House (1917) in Barnsdall Park and the Millard House (1923) in Pasadena (RIGHT), which was made of pierced concrete blocks with reinforced concrete fill.

AN EXPLOSION in design—Los Angeles-based

A RICH ARRAY OF OBJECTS for use in the home, garden, and industry — ceramics, glassware, metalcraft, hangings — both handcrafted and manufactured, are assembled every three years for the comprehensive California Design Show, held at Pasadena Art Museum. Largest of its kind in the West, the show attracts national and international attention for the range, freshness, and quality of its exhibits.

LOS ANGELES DESIGNERS, who comprise two-thirds of the 300 professionals earning a place in the juried show, are a versatile lot, as this potpourri shows. Assembled on the steps of Greene and Greene's Gamble house, this fraction of the local entries includes paper furniture (tea cart, chair, stool), indoor-outdoor lamps, clock, combination dresser and cradle, newspaper dispenser, toys, a sculptured female figure which is also a chest of drawers, and a bright red beach buggy made from a kit manufactured to fit a Volkswagen chassis.

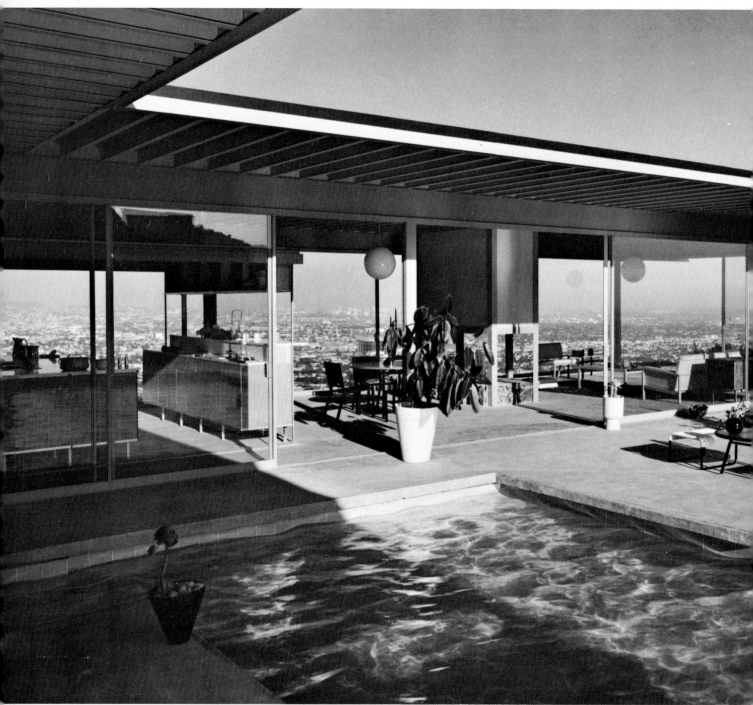

A STATEMENT IN STEEL, 1959 house by Pierre Koenig, built around a pool on top of a cliff, is one of several successful experiments using steel framing in home construction, resulting from Richard Neutra's long campaign to adapt commercial building techniques to homes.

FORERUNNERS in a new architectural idiom

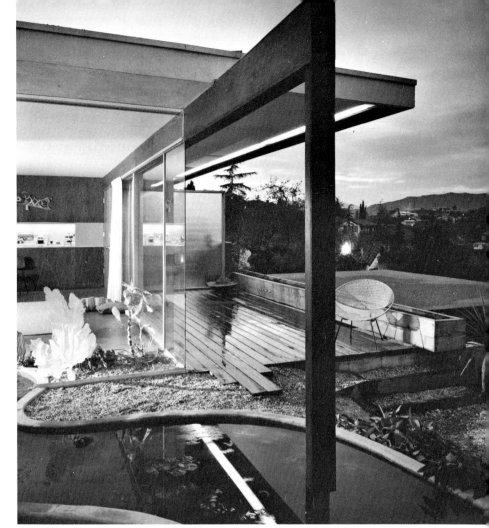

RICHARD NEUTRA, one of the foremost living architects, for forty years has been designing structures of an ageless warmth and simplicity, such as the 1955 Perkins house (ABOVE) in Pasadena, and building them with many technological "firsts" now taken for granted. Influential over a generation of architects, his mark can be seen in the work of many local designers. Earlier in time (BELOW), in fact too early for his own time, Irving Gill (1870–1936) abstracted the essence of the monumental California mission style and converted it to simple, severe but livable houses, such as the 1916 Dodge residence in West Hollywood.

205

SHORESIDE LIVING at the edge of the Pacific

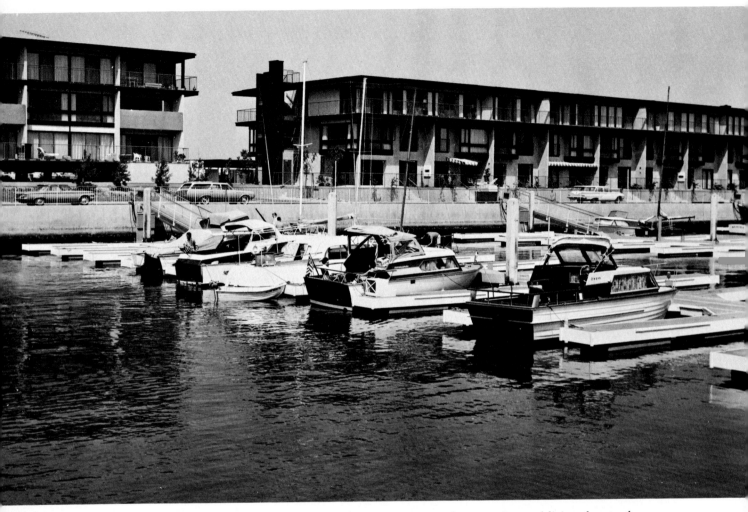

FOR BOAT OWNERS with salt water in their veins, the convenience of living close to the mooring dock is made possible by a choice of apartments — such as the complex at Marina del Rey (ABOVE) — villas, or island homes a few blocks away from dockage and yacht basins. In an area where waterfront lots sell for $150,000, marina apartments have special appeal; many are sold as condominiums, with boat care and pier maintenance provided by the group of apartment owners. Living right on the water's edge is only feasible in sheltered channels, free from tidal surge and protected from storm-driven waves.

FROM THE BLUFFS above Malibu, tile-roofed houses look out to sea, close enough for unobstructed view but far enough away from the ocean to escape the salt spray. The cluster of ranch-style homes is representative of the Spanish-influenced architecture prevalent in the region. The cool and substantial adobes of the 1830's were "discovered" in the early 1900's, rediscovered in 1915 when the Exposition at San Diego kindled interest in Spanish architecture, and have been an abiding model for succeeding generations of homeowners.

DAVID MUENCH

HIGH-RISE above the low horizon

DAVID MUENCH

RISING ABOVE THE FLAT SKYLINE, a scattering of high-rise structures viewed from the Hollywood Hills reveals the look of the future. Traditionally a sprawling city of single-family residences, four or five to an acre, Los Angeles is being forced to reach for the sky because of rising land values, disappearance of open country, and need for renewal of close-in areas. For 55 years, building heights in the city were limited to 150 feet or 13 stories (civic buildings excepted), but in 1956 a new law opened the way for unlimited heights, subject to controls to prevent congestion and keep population density low. The new buildings rise from spacious, parklike grounds, separated from their fellows and restricted to height districts. Between 1956–1966, 100 high-rise structures were built in Los Angeles; of those erected since World War II, 43 per cent are in downtown area, 32 per cent along Wilshire.

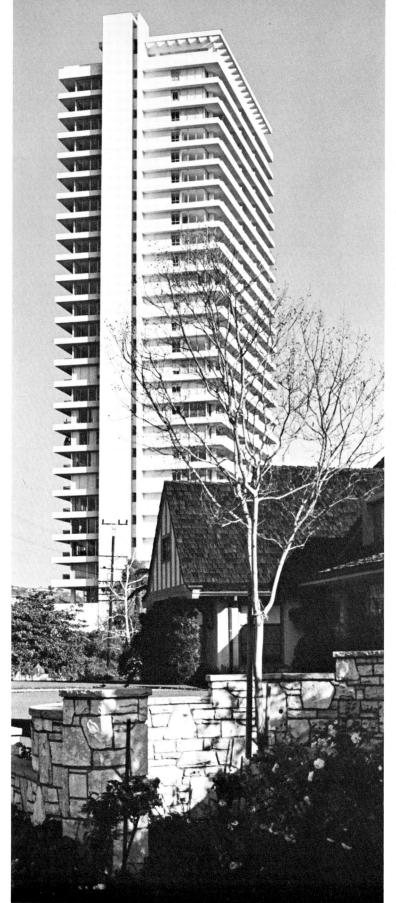

ROBERT BOBROW

HIGH-RISE APARTMENTS offer a number of saleable assets: view, sunlight and air, and amenities such as pools, saunas, rooftop gardens, internal parking. Because high-rise buildings legally are required to stand by themselves, they confront architects with the problem of creating a design that will stand scrutiny from all four sides and will survive years of exposure without becoming dated.

JULIUS SHULMAN

UNOBSTRUCTED BY other buildings, the view from the top can sweep over a hundred miles, as is true of the panorama from the 30th floor of Occidental Center (ABOVE), *site of a high-altitude restaurant and Japanese garden (foreground).*

PROBLEMS AND PLEASURES of living on a hillside

*SLANTING HILLSIDE SITES,
desirable because of the view or
elevation above the smog line, often
test home designers' skills. Some
architects, sidestepping the easy
answers of the bulldozer, match home
to site with daring. The three houses
by Richard Banta (RIGHT), hovering
over an "unbuildable" slope, are
essentially flat site houses, supported
on columns resting on deeply bedded
footings. The unusual "Chemosphere"
by John Lautner (BELOW) stands on a
single massive pillar with
radiating supports.*

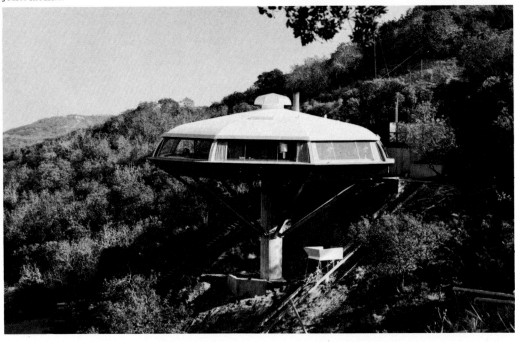

*SWIMMING POOLS in saturation characterize some of
the premium neighborhoods in the hill areas, such as
this square mile of homes near Sherman Oaks,
packed with 132 pools (not one of them occupied
when this photograph was taken).*

ART SHOW in the citadels of finance

LIKE THE MEDICI of Florence, bankers of Los Angeles have commissioned works of art to embellish their surroundings. The Lytton Center (ABOVE) is both headquarters of one of the nation's largest savings and loan associations and home of a first-rate gallery for California artists. A stained glass sculpture Spatial Kaleidoscope *(BELOW) revolves before a spotlight near the lobby, scattering splinters of colored light on the wall.*

LYTTON CENTER OF THE VISUAL ARTS

COPPER FOUNTAINS SPLASH in the shade of banks: Claire Falkenstein's Sculptured Water, *a fantasy of tubing and mist, cools the plaza of California Federal Savings, a loan association.*

Diversity on the Campus

Fresh winds rustle the ivy on 75 campuses; small colleges and giant universities offer a profusion of learning, some traditional, some highly experimental.

PREPLANNED UNIVERSITY, programmed to the year 2000

UNIVERSITY WITHIN A COMMUNITY: Starfish-shaped campus of the University of California at Irvine enjoys unique advantage of being developed within a master plan by William L. Pereira & Associates that embraces the surrounding 120 square miles. Its 1,000 acres (over twice the area of UCLA) is the core of a residential-commercial complex of 10,000 acres that is planned to grow in step with the university. By the turn of the century, the community is expected to have 100,000 people, the university 27,500 students. Commercial-residential districts intrude into the campus form, thanks to its unusual shape, permit interaction of town and gown.

COMMUNITY WITHIN THE UNIVERSITY: Buildings now standing give only a hint of the massive development planned for the Irvine campus. Heart of the plan is a central campus, formed around a ring with six major quadrangles shooting off like spokes, each devoted to a distinct academic field. With cars relegated to remote parking pastures, circulation will be by foot, bicycle, or elephant train. Ring connecting the quads is an underground utility channel, carrying heat, light, air-conditioning, television cables. Full advantage is taken of the commanding site of the campus, which will be landscaped with connecting parks.

REMINISCENT OF EARLY PHOTOGRAPHS of the first lonely buildings at UCLA and Berkeley standing in the midst of bean fields, the initial structures at University of California at Irvine rise in majestic isolation on a former cattle range. It takes little imagination to foresee the day when the open spaces will be filled—as at the other two campuses—with scores of buildings and peopled with thousands of bustling students.

JOHN WAGGAMAN

INSTITUTE of far-out technology

EARTHQUAKE'S SIGNATURE, scribed on revolving drums, is analyzed in Seismological Laboratory at the California Institute of Technology, Pasadena, one of the country's leading scientific colleges. Much of the present knowledge about earthquakes — of special relevance to quavery Californians—has been researched here under distinguished scientists. Concern with the technology of the here and now is a hallmark of Caltech, which combines technical training with a firm grounding in the humanities.

HOUSEFLY MEETS COMPUTER in a study of optics by students at Caltech. Battery of computers, available to all campus disciplines, typifies complex needs of a modern technical school.

216

SHADOW ON THE MOON is elongated image of Surveyor I, a robot spacecraft with its brains in Pasadena. Soft-landed on the moon in 1966 to photograph the lunar crust, it receives its commands from Caltech's Jet Propulsion Laboratory via telemetry. JPL was founded in 1936 by a handful of faculty and students hipped on rocketry, grew to eminence in space technology, and is now a facility of NASA, operated by Caltech. Although some graduate students and faculty members assist in its space probes, the laboratory is independent of the curriculum.

CLUSTER COLLEGE in Claremont

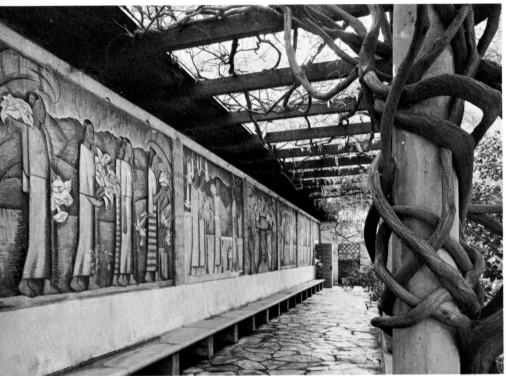

*MEXICAN MURAL graces a garden retreat on homelike campus
of Scripps College, one of the Claremont cluster. Each of the
colleges has its own architectural style, related to its educational
mission and controlled by a master plan that accommodates
extremes ranging from Pomona's Old Sumner (a remodeled hotel
from the 1880's) to the simple modernity of Harvey Mudd's
buildings.*

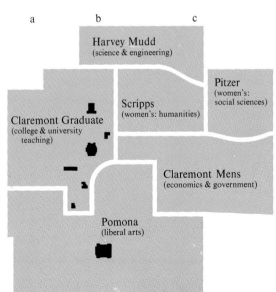

*JIGSAW OF CAMPUSES
grouped around common
facilities (indicated in black).
On the outskirts: A. Southern
California Theological School,
B. Rancho Santa Ana
Botanical Garden, and
C. future site of Immaculate
Heart College.*

a   b   c

Harvey Mudd
(science & engineering)

Pitzer
(women's:
social sciences)

Scripps
(women's: humanities)

Claremont Graduate
(college & university
teaching)

Claremont Mens
(economics & government)

Pomona
(liberal arts)

218

HIDDEN AMONG GROVES of oaks and eucalyptus are the six campuses of the Claremont Colleges, a group that combines the advantages of the small college with the facilities of a university. Each college retains its individuality, sets its own requirements, yet all share common library, research, laboratory, and entertainment facilities. Heart of the cluster is Pomona, a hard-to-enter college of the first rank, founded in 1887 at the time of the great land boom. Total enrollment for the five schools is under 4,000.

STAINLESS STEEL SCULPTURE formed by underwater explosion (ABOVE) *and megaliths of poured concrete* (BELOW) *entitled* Homage to Simon Rodia *are two of nine works of art on the campus of California State College at Long Beach, created by sculptors from seven nations at the invitation of the college. On several other campuses, permanent works of art are a prominent feature of the college environment; notably, sculpture at UCLA, modern stained-glass windows at Occidental, murals at Claremont.*

ART IN LIFE: an affirmation on two campuses

WITH BRIGHT BANNERS held aloft, crowd waits for the cadence of bagpipes and recorders to start the Mary's Day parade, a joyous happening that bursts upon the campus of Immaculate Heart College every spring. Using the vivid colors of the marketplace, mixing advertising slogans with scriptural quotations, art students create scores of pennants and ponchos for the celebration. The college affirms the belief that art — like modern technology — knows no boundaries, and the art faculty, including internationally-known artist Sister Mary Corita, encourages students to make it a part of everyday living and to seek beauty and truth in homely — even crassly commercial — things.

CHILDREN'S CLINIC IN TIJUANA, Mexico, comes rapidly together (ABOVE) under assault of a student crew, and (BELOW) culturally handicapped children in Los Angeles receive tutoring as part of a program in community service at Occidental College that brings more than 200 students face to face with ignorance, non-motivation and poverty. In exchange for helping hundreds of young people less privileged than they, the students stretch their own learning horizons far beyond the campus boundaries. Occidental (founded 1887), one of a scattering of high-quality colleges in the area, is a selective school, has had a full share of Rhodes Scholars and National Merit Scholars.

STUDENTS PEERING OVER BERLIN
wall and waiting for a bus at The Hague
(LEFT) are on tour from the Whittier College
campus in Copenhagen. As part of the
semester's study, students tour Europe when
they arrive in fall, visit West Berlin
at mid-term.

WHITTIER COLLEGE, founded in 1901 by the Quakers, was
one of the first colleges in the United States to open a campus
abroad. Since 1959, the college has been offering an opportunity
for qualified upperclassmen to broaden their awareness of the
world around them by enrolling for a semester of classroom study
at the University of Copenhagen. Other local colleges also offer
European study, but on an individual scholarship basis.

A CITY OF LEARNING within a city

CRANES AND BULLDOZERS are a way of life on the 411-acre campus of the University of California at Los Angeles, which has grown in one generation from a cluster of five Romanesque buildings on a hilltop in 1929 (ABOVE) to the city of learning at the right. Since the end of World War II, a $160 million building program has been under way to house a university program of incredible magnitude and diversity. Overlaying standard academic fare are disciplines in space science and computerized research, cultural activities in such profusion that they make the university a major force in the city's cultural life, plus an athletic program of such prowess that its teams are respected in all sports. Started as a normal school in 1881, it became a branch of the state university in 1919.

THE UNIVERSITY FAMILY consists of 29,000 students (from the top eighth of the state's high school graduates), 2,000 faculty members, 375 teaching assistants, and 675 researchers, distributed among 71 departments in 14 schools and colleges.

CREATIVE CINEMA, bright star in USC's academic firmament

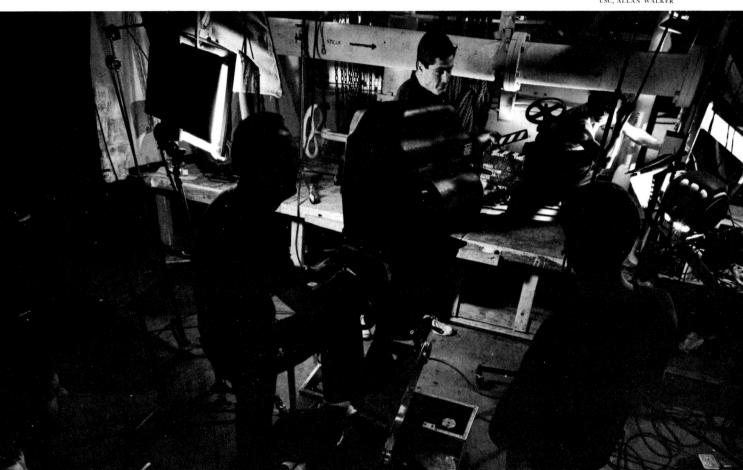

*A SENIOR CREW shooting scenes for a class project (*ABOVE*) and a film editor working through the night (*LEFT*) are common sights in the Department of Cinema at the University of Southern California. One of USC's excellent professional disciplines, cinema is a full major with graduate courses leading to advanced degrees. Oldest (1929), largest, and best-known school of the film in the country, it attracts more students from other states and abroad than from California. Started with the help of Hollywood producers, it is actively supported by leading professionals. Most graduates enter commercial, educational, or governmental cinema; some have made outstanding reputations in Hollywood.*

HONORED AT THE EDINBURGH Film Festival, "The Dominator" and "The Face of Lincoln" are two of many USC-produced films that are winning awards for excellence abroad and in this country.

The Transplanted Landscape

*Like its people, most of the plant materials flourishing
in Los Angeles' gardens and parks started life somewhere
else, emigrated from the four corners of the globe.*

A FORESTED RETREAT in central Los Angeles

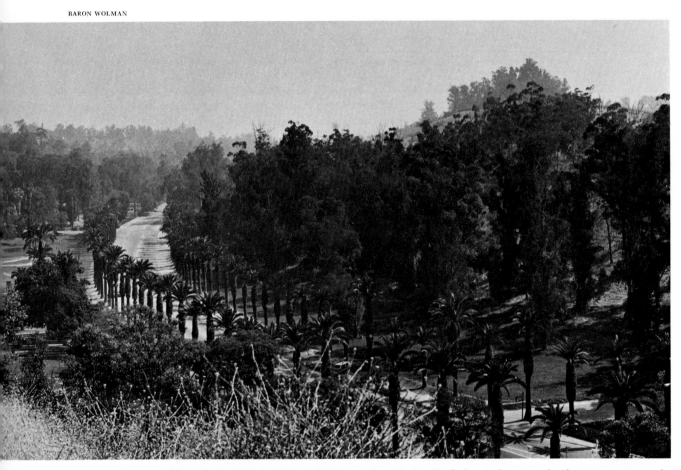

*THE CITY SEEMS FAR AWAY in sylvan Elysian Park, located next to the downtown area and a
stone's throw from Dodger Stadium. Occupying land set aside for the original Pueblo, the park
was created officially in the 1880's and part of its rugged acreage was assigned to experimental
planting. First botanical garden in Southern California, Elysian contains hundreds of unusual
trees and shrubs, planted over a 30-year period. Stadium Way (ABOVE) curves between files of rare
wild date palms from India, set out at the turn of the century, at the lower end of the Chavez
Ravine arboretum. The Ravine (RIGHT) has plantings from the world over. Australia is
represented by the eucalyptus forest in the background and New Zealand by the lofty kauri pine
framed by California palms.*

FLOURISHING EXOTICS from the other side of the world

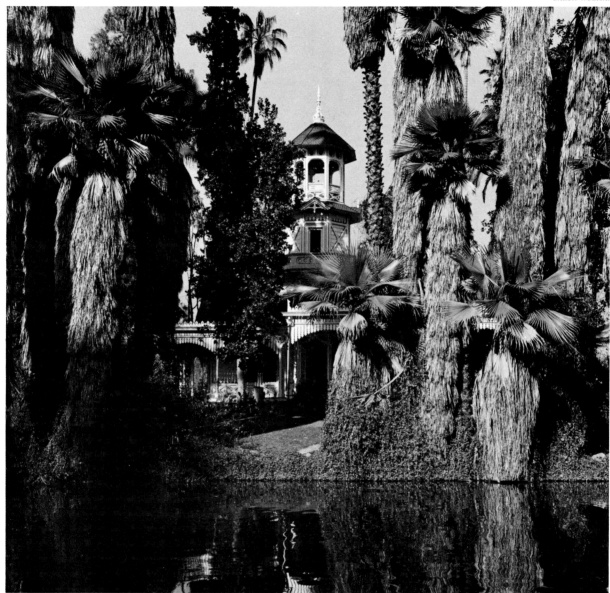

JUNGLE PLANTS were imported in 1880's to please a flamboyant silver baron, Lucky Baldwin, who also built the rococo Queen Anne guest cottage standing among the palms. The lush tropical plantings around the rim of the natural lagoon are part of a remarkable collection of exotics test grown at the State and County Arboretum at Arcadia. Nearby, a demonstration garden sponsored jointly with Sunset Magazine *displays take-home ideas in garden design.*

A JAPANESE TEA PAVILION nestles in a camellia forest in La Canada at Descanso Gardens, which are public. A relative of the commercial tea plant, the camellia is half-a-world away from its native home, the coast of China and the islands offshore, but it shares the cultural needs of the native California oak and thrives under its shade and leaf fall.

THE TRANSPLANTED LANDSCAPE 231

ONE OF THE WORLD'S
great gardens in San Marino

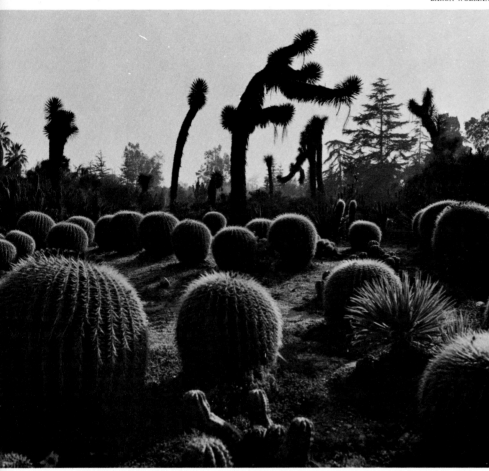

*CACTI OF FASCINATING and implausible form fill
ten acres of the celebrated desert garden in the
Henry E. Huntington Botanical Gardens. The 1,500
species were imported from the world's arid regions and
represent the largest collection anywhere of mature
desert plants growing out-of-doors.*

*AN ASSEMBLAGE OF 17TH-CENTURY statuary from Padua,
stationed against an evergreen backdrop, gives an air of old world formality
to the North Vista. Although begun 60 years ago without a master plan,
the 200-acre estate has a unity and maturity uncommon in botanical
gardens. Most of the plants were mature specimens when they were moved
in, and they were set out to best display their landscaping values.
Noteworthy collections: five-acre camellia garden (1,200 varieties), plants
from Shakespeare, an idyllic Japanese poolside garden, orange and
first commercial avocado grove in California.*

232   THE TRANSPLANTED LANDSCAPE

A JAPANESE garden of rare beauty and authenticity

DARROW WATT

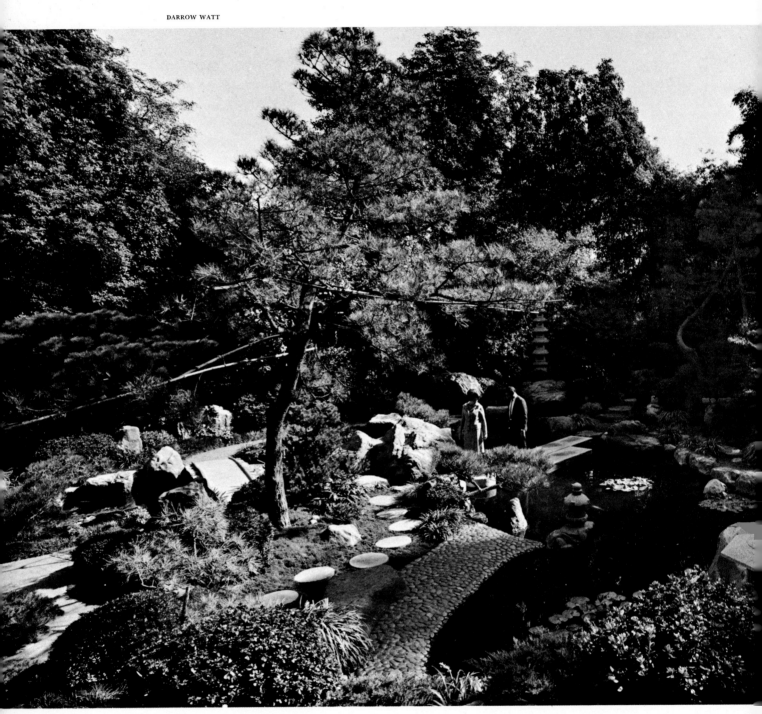

"PEACE FOR THE EYE and spirit," is the way the chancellor of UCLA described the university's exquisite Japanese garden tucked away in Bel Air. Designed to be walked through, the garden delights the stroller with miniature compositions of stone, wood, and plants that evoke natural scenes. Its design, most of its structure, rocks, and lamps came from Japan. Magically, it looks older (installed 1962), larger (acre-plus) than it is.

BARK-ROOFED SHRINE in highest section is nailless, rests free on foundation stones. White pebbles set in cement (BELOW) symbolize torrent of water flowing under the teahouse. Pebbles are small where the water would be most turbulent, large where it would be placid. Designed in elaborate Kyoto style, the garden is a research facility, open to the public only on occasion.

Fruits from the Mediterranean

MAX YAVNO

*Fruits and field crops from Spain and Italy, some planted
by mission padres, were once mainstay of local economy,
still make region among top agricultural areas in country.*

SWEET WINE country, a century under the sun

ERNEST BRAUN

*A MILLION GALLONS of wine age below ground level at Brookside Winery in the Cucamonga
area (immortalized by Jack Benny). A dozen wineries, two over a century old, produce a variety
of brands (BELOW), mostly dessert wines. Oldest crop in the state, wine grapes were planted by
Franciscan fathers at San Gabriel in 1804 and crushed under Indian feet. The harsh mission
wine was the staple for nearly 50 years before better rootstocks yielded more potable fare. The
wine-producing area is shrinking in face of urban growth, but 19,000 acres are still occupied by
great sweeping vineyards, such as Virginia Dare (RIGHT).*

MISSION OLIVES, tasty heritage from Spain

SINCE BIBLICAL DAYS, olives have been leached in a bath of water, alkali, or "secret formula" to remove the glucosides that make the fruit too bitter even for birds. If cured without exposure to air, olives come out green; if exposed, they turn black, sometimes accelerated with iron coloring. Olives curing (ABOVE) at Graber's in Ontario are from century-old trees.

ALL OF AMERICA'S OLIVES are grown in the West, most of them in the Los Angeles area. Part of the Spanish heritage, trees were planted at the missions before 1800. All commercial groves, such as the ones at Sylmar (ABOVE), were propagated from mission cuttings, now supplemented with other varieties that yield larger fruit. The tender olives are hand-harvested when straw yellow — the tree-ripened, black olives are too soft for processing.

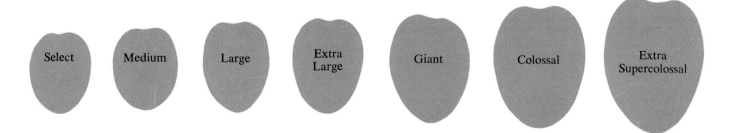

AMUSING SIZE DESIGNATIONS have sensible explanation. First olives marketed (mission) were classed small, medium, large. *Later varieties had bigger fruit, required new terms larger than* large, *hence the ascending superlatives.*

FRUITS FROM THE MEDITERRANEAN 239

HOUSEWIVES IN 80 foreign lands, where the name Sunkist is a household word, and throughout the United States (including Florida) are reminded frequently of the virtues of the citrus products marketed by the Los Angeles based cooperative, founded in 1893. Sunkist advertisements above sell a citrus drink and lemons in Denmark and France.

SUNKIST PHOTO

HISTORIC ADVERTISEMENT, a full page in two colors in the Des Moines Register and Leader in 1908, was part of an experimental campaign to determine if advertising would increase sales of oranges then piling up in Southern California. As part of the test, fruit was shipped to Iowa in bannered cars, prize contests were held, and billboards proclaimed "Oranges for Health — California for Wealth." Result: sale of oranges in Iowa increased 50 per cent, and Sunkist was launched on an aggressive advertising career that has never let up.

ORANGE GROWERS learned after costly trial and error that citrus grew best in foothills above the frost line. Precise groves set out on the hills west of Pomona (RIGHT) proved less vulnerable to frostburn than those on the flat, where the main protection was the towering eucalyptus windbreak and the sooty smudgepots.

WILLIAM GARNETT

Innovative Industry

*Major manufacturing center of the West,
Los Angeles produces in unfettered
variety; dominated by three old-timers—
aircraft, petroleum, movies—and their
glamorous offspring.*

FINANCIER TO an expanding economy

ERNEST BRAUN

*A JUMPING PLACE during the morning hours when
it is in action, the Stock Exchange at 6th and Spring
Streets transacts an annual $1 billion in stock transfers,
has 128 members, and lists 600 local and nationally
known securities. Activity reflects vigor of the financial
growth of the area, which was once wholly dependent on
outside capital but is now capable of financing a
substantial portion of its own development, ranks third
in the nation as a banking center. Because of sprawling
growth, area has pioneered in branch banking, now has
more than 700 branch banks in Los Angeles County
alone. Also in the financial picture, competing for the
dollars of the thrifty, are savings and loan associations,
which now hold 10 per cent of all savings and loan
assets in the country.*

OIL FOR 4 million thirsty cars

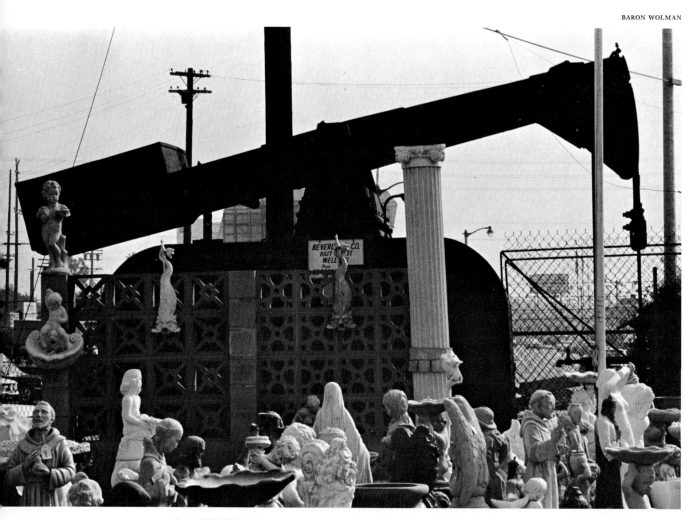

GRASSHOPPER OIL PUMP, nodding tirelessly amid garden statuary on Beverly Boulevard, is one of thousands spotted throughout Los Angeles. These picturesque pumps gradually are being displaced in urban areas by more discreet installations hidden underground, in basements, garages, simulated office buildings, and landscaped parks, in an effort by the oil industry to improve the aesthetic appeal of its drilling and pumping equipment. Despite the quantity of wells sucking away at the underground reservoir, the oil industry is unable to quench the thirst of the four million cars in the county, and it has to import crude from the Central Valley or overseas. In 1940, the industry produced twice as much crude as the county could consume; now, it falls short by a third. Still, petroleum is a major industry in the county, which ranks second in the state in crude production.

CAMOUFLAGED OIL RIGS on three tropical islands represent the industry's ingenious answer to the problem of tapping the oil pool under Long Beach harbor without spoiling the seascape of the "Riviera of the West." Disguised as high-rise apartments, the rigs drill myriads of slanting, mile-deep holes. Oil is piped from the islands to refineries. In time, the islands will be graced with 30-foot waterfalls and clusters of giant abstract sculptures.

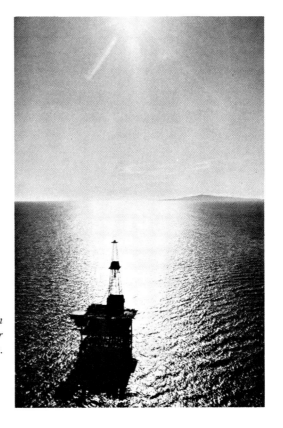

LONELY OIL RIG, standing on piling in the open sea, is an earlier approach to offshore drilling.

245

INNOVATION is commonplace in aerospace

MAURICE E. MANSON

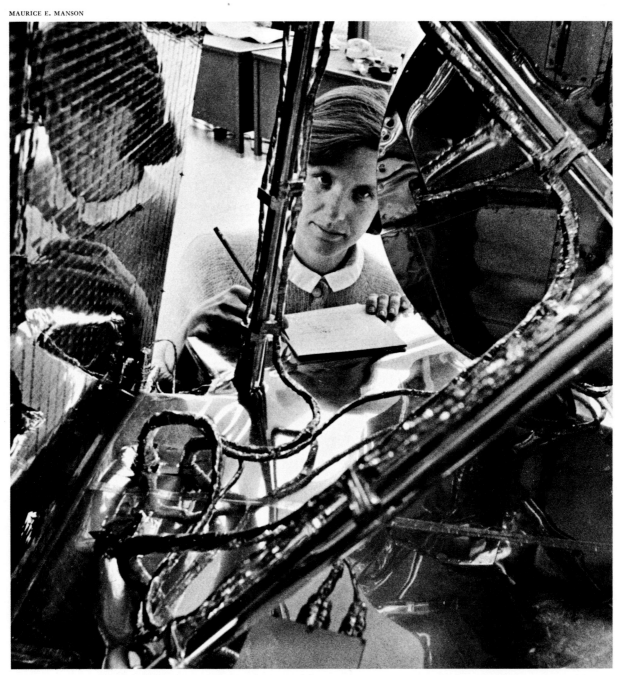

NOVEL MACHINERY, NEW FACES, strange sights and sounds are taken for granted in the aerospace industry. The glistening mockup of Venus satellite, Mariner II, elegant as a piece of kinetic sculpture, is checked out by physicist Marcia Neugebauer, Woman Scientist of the Year (1967), who designed its instrumentation for measuring solar winds. On the days when Lockheed tests rocket engines in the hills back of Redlands (RIGHT), windows rattle for miles around. The towering plume was produced by a solid propellant rocket with a thrust of 3 million pounds, enough to place a flight of 50 small Volkswagens in orbit around the earth.

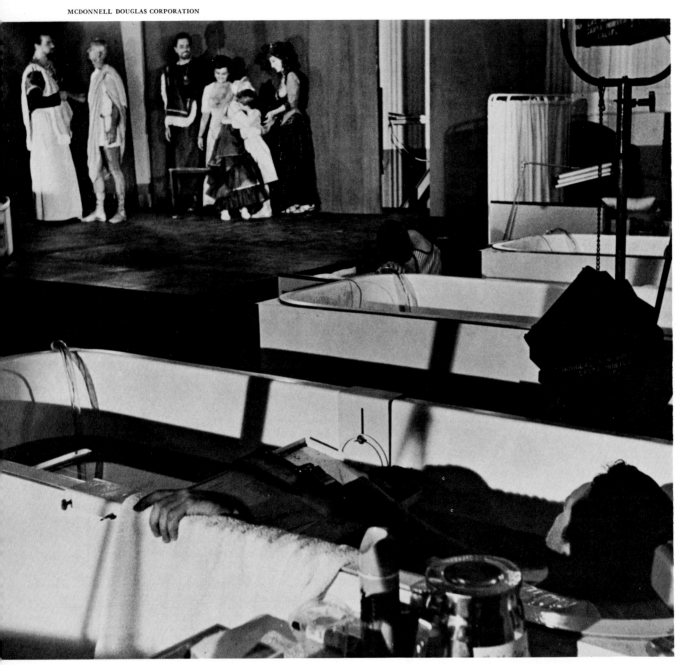

SHAKESPEARE'S "WINTER'S TALE," performed in the unlikely surroundings of a biotechnical laboratory by a Hollywood workshop group, relieves the tedium for college students floating in tubs of silicone oil at McDonnell Douglas. The men were engaged in a marathon bath of ten days' duration followed by ten days in bed, in a NASA experiment to determine which medium — oil bath or bed rest — best simulated the conditions of weightlessness to be encountered in extended interplanetary travel.

FAMILIAR FORM of the
*Apollo capsule was duplicated
at North American in an
oven-freezer combination that
tested the vehicle's resistance
to heat and cold. The device
produces temperatures from
plus 600° to minus 320°F.*

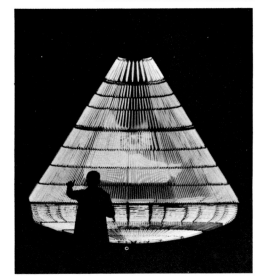

*ON ITS WAY TO THE MOON, a Surveyor
vehicle in its white crate is accompanied by
ten times its weight in instruction manuals
as it is loaded aboard a specially built air
freighter bound for Cape Kennedy. These
lunar vehicles are the imposing communal
product of hundreds of subcontractors
working under Hughes Aircraft and
coordinated by California Institute
of Technology.*

EXPLORING the final frontier—Ocean Space

LOCKHEED

DEEP QUEST, a 50-ton research submarine designed to carry a 7,000-pound payload more than a mile beneath the sea, takes final form in the shops of Lockheed's missile and space division. Adapting techniques learned in developing self-contained environments for astronauts and jet pilots, several aerospace firms are experimenting with ways that men can live and work on the bottom of the ocean. Working with the Navy, oil companies, and universities, the industry is exploring the dark depths of Ocean Space, the final frontier, with its vast possibilities as a resource for food, drugs, and mineral wealth, and its potential as a refuge for the navies of the future.

NORTH AMERICAN ROCKWELL CORPORATION

BEAVER IV, a work submarine, undergoes wind-tunnel tests at North American Rockwell before it goes into production. Designed to operate down to 2,000 feet, the compact submersible will carry frogmen down to oil well sites, rescue missions, or will transfer men to undersea habitats. Mechanical arms controlled from inside enable it to accomplish some tasks without committing men to the water. It will be based at USC's marine laboratory on Catalina Island.

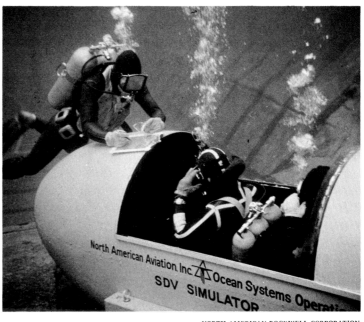

A "WET" SUBMARINE, being tested in a tank, will transport scuba divers and their tools to underwater worksites, relieving the men of the muscular effort and wasted oxygen consumed in swimming to and from work.

NORTH AMERICAN ROCKWELL CORPORATION

JETLINERS for the peaceful skies

PLANE-LOAD OF PASSENGERS, 251 of them, converge on a Super 61 Douglas DC-8, fresh from the production line of the McDonnell Douglas Corporation in Long Beach. An early entry in the jumbo jet series, the plane is the largest commercial jetliner built in the region. One of the four plane builders in the area that make Los Angeles County a major aircraft production center, Douglas got its start in the 1920's with military contracts. During World War II, the firm expanded enormously, becoming the world's largest producer of aircraft and the fourth largest industry in the nation. After the war, the company concentrated on commercial airliners, continuing a series already launched in 1934 with the fabulous DC-3, and later, following the industry trend, branched out into missiles and aerospace.

RARE SIGHT: commercial jets flying in formation. These four Douglas DC-9's were photographed in test flight prior to their introduction in 1966. Each plane was loaded with five tons of instrumentation and recording apparatus. The tail-engined craft was designed for fast, short haul flights.

MCDONNELL DOUGLAS CORPORATION

WORKERS JOIN the nose to the 187-foot fuselage of a stretched-out (by 37 feet) and re-engineered version of the DC-8, familiar to every patron of the airways.

INNOVATIVE INDUSTRY 253

SUPERSONIC AIRCRAFT—the sound of tomorrow

LOCKHEED

WORLD'S FASTEST AIRCRAFT in flight above the desert, a twin-engine delta-wing interceptor, the YF-12A, is one of a sequence of innovative planes developed by Lockheed Aircraft Corporation, Burbank. The titanium craft, which cruises above 80,000 feet at more than 2,000 miles an hour, was the first aircraft to fly three times the speed of sound, holds eight world speed records. It contributed to development of Lockheed's spy plane, the SR-71, which can survey 60,000 square miles in an hour's flight. Lockheed started in 1913, moved to Burbank in 1928 and reorganized in 1932, has made notable contributions to aircraft design, including a speedy revolutionary rigid-rotor helicopter.

WORLD'S LARGEST SUPERSONIC, long-range plane, the XB-70A research aircraft was designed and built by the Los Angeles division of North American Rockwell. The enormous plane, shown with wing tips lowered in supersonic flight, has flown 2,000 miles an hour at 70,000 feet, embodies a new generation of aeronautical advances, has accumulated data of great value in the coming Age of the Supersonic Transport. One of two prototypes, its twin was lost in a tragic accident during a photographic mission. North American (founded 1928) also is producing fighter and reconnaissance planes, is working in nuclear power, electronics, and laser communications systems.

INNOVATIVE INDUSTRY 255

NORTH AMERICAN ROCKWELL CORPORATION

MOTION PICTURES, a complex cross of art and business

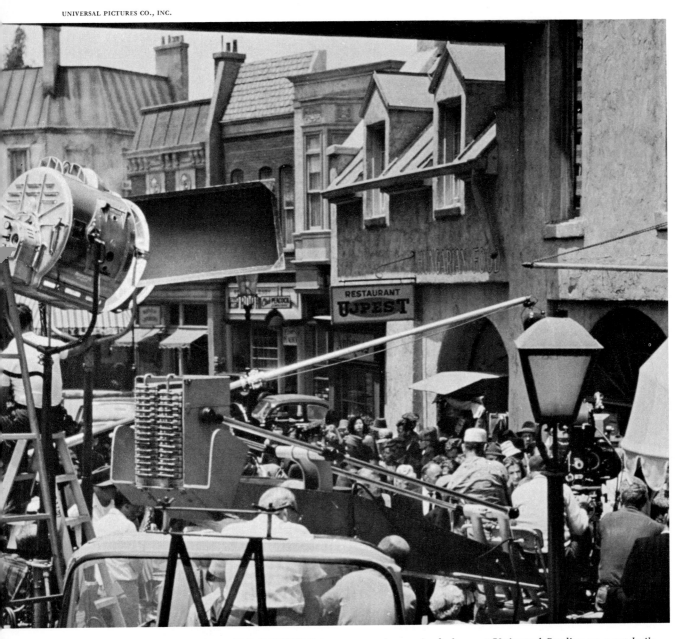

CAMERAS ARE ROLLING in a scene of organized chaos at Universal Studios on a set built in 1923 for the "Hunchback of Notre Dame" and since refurbished for a hundred pictures. Basic techniques of filming have changed little since the pioneers first turned the crank here (1915) in the perpetual sunshine, but movie making has become increasingly complex, and a modern film requires services of a dozen distinct specialties. (RIGHT) *Launching of a major film at Grauman's Chinese in Hollywood has been a grandiose custom since 1927 when the "temple of the cinema" was dedicated with a "$5,000,000 event." On this night, Norma Talmadge accidentally stepped in wet concrete and started a tradition of recording foot and handprints that has become what one writer calls one of the "quasi-paleontological sights of the region."*

INNOVATIVE INDUSTRY   257

THE ARTFUL INDUSTRY of make-believe—illusion by the acre

THE LATENT SCHIZOPHRENIC in anyone is likely to be stirred by the mesmerizing blend of reality and unreality in the great movie set compounds, such as this one at Universal Studios, the setting for countless movies. This elaborate complex burned to the ground a few weeks after this photograph was taken, but it was largely rebuilt to avoid refilming the half-dozen pictures then being made within the compound.

*OFFSHOOT OF BOTH the movies and television, record making (*ABOVE*) is a major industry, ranking in dollar volume with the women's wear business. Recording sessions, such as actor David McCallum recording "98.6," are cluttered, informal, monitored by an army of technicians.*

IN THE FIRST WILD years of television, the motion picture industry nearly collapsed. From 700 films a year, Hollywood dropped to less than 300, half of them shot abroad. Theaters closed, studios merged and submerged, some never to surface again. Now, over 80 per cent of filming done in Hollywood is for television, and more network shows originate here than in New York. Techniques for televising, as in the Danny Kaye scene (ABOVE), often force performers to work in cramped space because of the limited area of the television screen. Actors work hemmed in by bulky recording equipment and gaggles of spotlights.

THE LUSTY OFFSPRING that almost killed Hollywood

Gateway to the World

Newest of major Western ports, the harbor leads in tonnage, in modern handling techniques; home of the Navy, tuna fleet, the super-supertanker.

TWIN PORTS share a watery maze

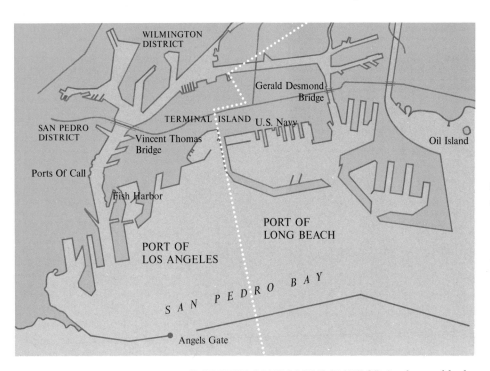

LARGEST MAN-MADE HARBOR *in the world, the maze of channels, inlets, and islands covers 50 miles of developed waterfront, shielded by a nine-mile breakwater. Operations are split between Los Angeles and Long Beach (see map) that divide jurisdiction, nearly duplicate each other's facilities, and compete mercilessly. Between the two of them, they have made the port the West coast leader in tonnage. Port of Long Beach, floating over a pool of oil, is subsidized partly by oil royalties; Los Angeles is completely self-sustaining.*

FRANK GORE

HOME PORT for men of war

WITH EVERY PERCH OCCUPIED by sailors eager to disembark, a cruiser ties up at the naval shipyard in Long Beach Harbor after a long voyage. War vessels are a common sight in the port, but only the Coast Guard cutters are permanent residents, the remainder are in transit, stopping off for repairs or modernization. Long Beach is a major repair facility for the 11th Naval District based in San Diego. When several large ships are docked at the port, the flood of sailors on shore leave added to those employed in the naval facilities around the harbor give downtown Long Beach the restless air of a navy town.

"LONG HENRY", *gigantic floating crane dwarfs its companions in naval shipyard. One of three built by Germany for Russia, it was seized in World War II and brought from Kiel to Long Beach disassembled. One mate went to Russia; other was lost at sea on its way to England. Largest floating crane in world (along with Russian twin), it can lift a locomotive without strain.*

DOUBLE CHRISTENING, by widow and granddaughter of admiral for whom the ship is named, launches the destroyer escort Hepburn *down the ways at Todd Shipyards, largest of the nine in Los Angeles Harbor engaged in the multi-million dollar business of building and renovating everything from catamarans to yachts to freighters.*

EXPORT-IMPORT, the two-way cornucopia

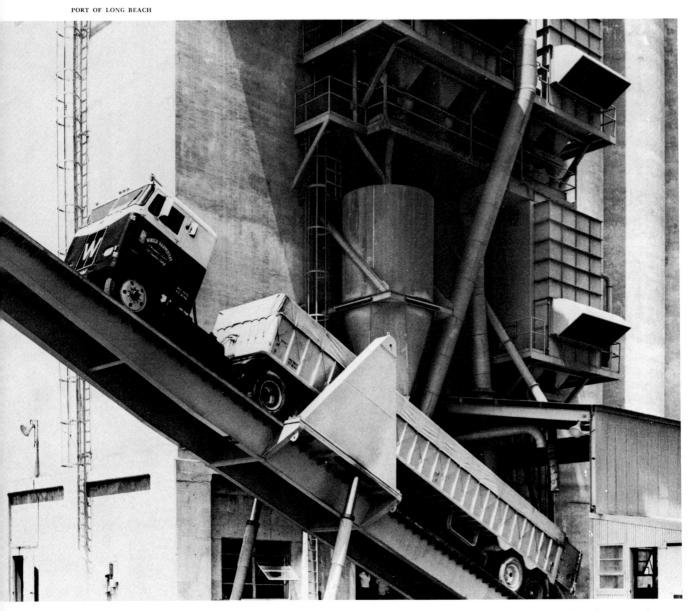

EXPORTS: Truckload of grain empties itself in a few minutes in Long Beach terminal. Ingenious rig is typical of both ports' modern cargo-handling facilities that tilt, shake, up-end, dump, suck, compress, munch, package, magnetize a variety of raw and finished products for export, including cotton, oranges, squashed cars, milk, animal feeds, old clothes, potash, coke, iron-ore pellets, railroad axles, old newspapers, and, surprisingly, the original cargo that launched the harbor in the Spanish period: hides and tallow. Value of cargo handled today through the two ports amounts to $3 billion a year.

IMPORTS: Regiments of Volkswagens, freshly disembarked from their own vessel, are recurrent sight in port of Los Angeles. Other imports from 200 harbors: bananas, Mexican salt, pipe, Scotch whiskey, petroleum, copra, newsprint, crude rubber, plate glass, cameras, and a pair of white rhinoceroses named Wink and Pink.

PRIDE of two harbors

MAJESTIC QUEEN MARY, gliding inexorably through a sea of welcoming craft, heads for her final berth alongside Pier J in Long Beach Harbor, December 9, 1967. Once the largest and fastest passenger vessel afloat, the Queen Mary *became a financial liability to its owners, the Cunard Steamship Company Ltd., and was sold to the city of Long Beach for $3,450,000 to be re-outfitted as a maritime museum and a posh hotel and restaurant complex. The legendary vessel, launched in 1934, was queen of the seas during her years on the transatlantic run. During World War II, she carried three-quarters of a million troops abroad, 15,000 per trip, at such a speed (28 knots) that she never needed a convoy and was able to elude the wolfpacks of U-boats.*

HANDSOME SUSPENSION BRIDGE, painted an iridescent green, connects Terminal Island with San Pedro, arches 185 feet above the main channel. Named for a prominent local legislator, Vincent Thomas, it was dedicated in 1963. Third largest suspension bridge in the state, it resembles a scaled-down version of the Golden Gate Bridge.

Statistics	Feet
Center span	*1,500*
Side spans	*500*
Height above water	*185*
Height of towers	*365*
Total length	*6,060*

Imaginative Merchandising

For the pleasure and ease of the shopper, beguiling surroundings in the marketplace: plazas, malls, fountains and pinwheels — and goods from everywhere.

THE MALL IDEA: planting grass in Main Street

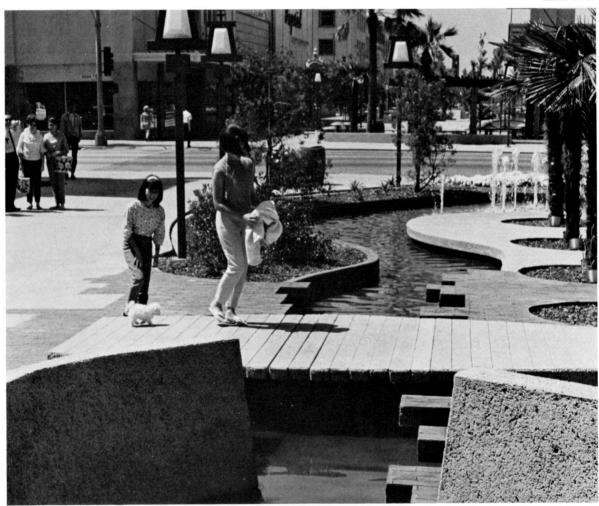

LANDSCAPED MALLS have returned excitement and activity to downtown shopping areas that have suffered from a drain of customers to outlying shopping centers. The ideas behind the mall are simple: bar autos from the area but provide ample parking nearby, and introduce imaginative landscaping to make it a pleasant shopping place, such as the Riverside Mall above. Nearly half of the shopping malls in the country are in the Los Angeles area.

PLEASANTLY STIMULATING places, malls are graced with a profusion of plant material, cooling sight and sound of running water, benches for the weary or sociable, and fanciful bridges, fountains, sidewalk games, trash receptacles. Riverside (ABOVE). Pomona (BELOW) was the pioneer.

OLVERA STREET—the West's
first shopping mall

REMINDER OF THE DAY when Los
Angeles was a bustling Mexican pueblo,
block-long Olvera Street evokes the
light-hearted air of a Mexican village with
its open booths and cafes and its bright
confusion of souvenirs, handicrafts, and
objects of art. A highly successful enterprise,
the street in downtown Los Angeles was
rescued from grimy oblivion by
public-spirited citizens in 1929 and
converted to what is probably the West's
first shopping mall.

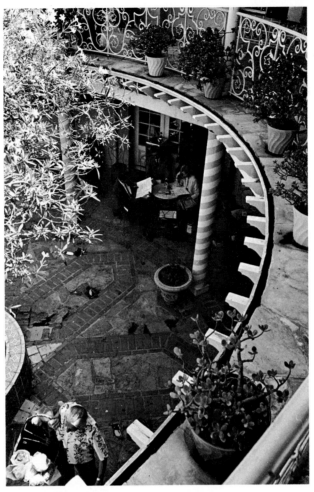

REFRESHMENT STOP *in one of the four patio restaurant-shops in Westwood Village shopping area, noted for array of candlemakers, jewelsmiths, tobacconists, art shops.*

ANTIQUE MOVIE *posters and rare comic books are features of a collectors bookstore, the most specialized in a concentration of bookstores along Hollywood Boulevard that has made the area equivalent to bookshop districts in New York and London. In three miles, between Western and La Brea avenues, there are 20 bookstores on the boulevard or within a block or two.*

FOODS OF THE WORLD excite the eyes and the nose in the cavernous Grand Central Market (317 Broadway), a block-deep indoor food bazaar that attracts some 200,000 customers a week. The market has so many Spanish-speaking customers that stalls have bilingual signs and sales people. An outdoor counterpart in western Los Angeles, Farmer's Market (3rd and Fairfax) also offers massed displays of produce. Grown from a handful of stalls in a vacant field in 1934, market now has 160 owner-operated stalls, shops, restaurants.

ENDLESS VARIETY in the marketplace

PLEASURABLE SHOPPING in opulent surroundings

BEGUILING BAZAARS at their best, shopping centers feature tasteful architectural design control, landscaped malls and plazas (pioneered in 1950's by Bullock's Fashion Squares), and parking prairies banished to the periphery. At Fashion Island Shopping Center, Irvine Ranch, featured on these pages, the master designers (Welton Becket and Associates) have lavished care on the parklike landscaping. A zigzag mall runs between staggered rows of stores, and branching from it are a half dozen plazas, each designed for a special function. In one (BELOW), a cluster of shops is situated on a small island reached by stepping stones across a lily pond.

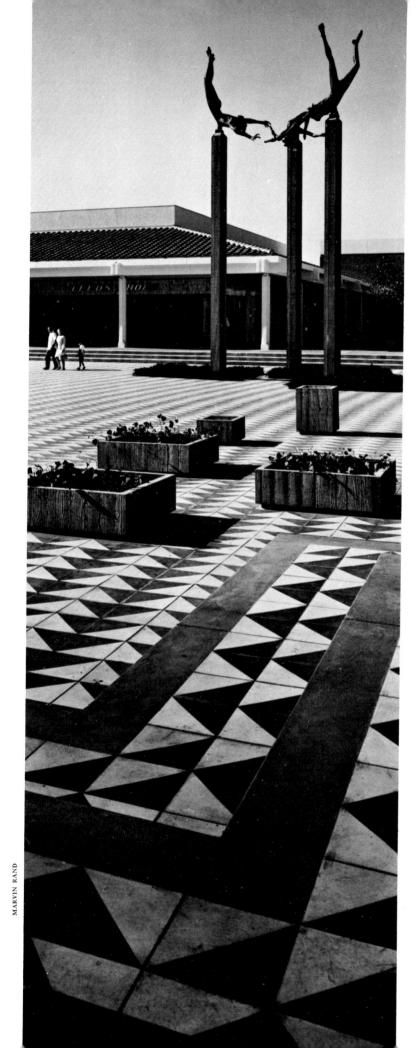

THREE COURT JESTERS balancing overhead (LEFT) dominate a sunken square paved with blue and white tiles and designed for special exhibitions and open-air performances. A play plaza for children (ABOVE) is equipped with playground apparatus and distractions such as an oversize multicolor pinwheel, a spinning dish, amusing fountains, and a resonant bridge that reverberates when children run across it. These are two of the seven plazas designed with wit and style by Sasaki-Walker Associates.

277

New City Forms

To serve a city of cities, government and commerce follow new forms, collecting in scattered pockets or stretching out along the boulevards and freeways.

ORIGINAL SEAT of civic power, still the biggest of all

DAVID MUENCH

*LARGEST CONCENTRATION of public buildings
outside of Washington, D.C., the Los Angeles Civic
Center complex employs more office workers and spends
more billions of dollars than several state capitals. For
35 years, the City Hall (LEFT) was the principal
landmark, towering 32 stories above the low-roofed city,
but its dominance has been eclipsed by the dramatic
Water and Power Building (ABOVE) standing squarely at
the head of the great mall in company with the Music
Center pavilions. A vast, airy building, W&P can be seen
for miles at night, for it is always fully lit. Strollers circle
its ground-level promenade (RIGHT) taking in the view
and cooling off in the spray from the fountains
that rise from reflecting pools, part
of the building's air-conditioning system.*

NEW AND OLD fashions in civic centers

FRESH ARCHITECTURAL STYLING of library in Pomona is dictated by over-all design concepts in master plan for a new civic center that is one of several blossoming as a result of the expanding role of the intertwined local and county governments. Some of the newer centers provide for the welfare of workers and patrons with features such as the concrete picnic booths (LEFT) lining the mall of the branch civic center in West Los Angeles. In summer, employees lunch here, and in the evenings, concerts and folk dances take over a paved square around a roofed bandstand.

LIKE A EUROPEAN PALACE, the Pasadena City Hall dominates a spacious brick-paved square. Though over-decorated and inconvenient by today's standards, the building conveys a feeling of permanence and integrity. Pride of the 1920's, it was built during a Spanish architectural revival that also produced the Beverly Hills City Hall.

A LINEAL CITY: opulent Wilshire Boulevard

WALTER HOUK

MONUMENTAL SCULPTURE, *dominating inner court of a medical center west of Bixel Street, is one of the many works of art that enhances the groundspace of some of the newer buildings along Wilshire. At last count, there were 18 fountains (mostly on the south side of the street), 25 pieces of sculpture (mostly on the north side), and innumerable mosaic and enamel pieces spread out along the length of the boulevard.*

DAN BUDNIK

L.A. TIMES

FANCIFUL PREDICTION in 1927 of Wilshire Boulevard of the future. In the 1920's, Wilshire pioneered these "firsts": ornamental street lighting, synchronized traffic lights, parking limits, Christmas street decorations, crosstown bus service, district trade show.

TOWERS OF WILSHIRE cast long shadows in the late afternoon sun that highlights the canyonlike character of the boulevard stretching 16 miles from downtown Los Angeles to the ocean. One of the world's prestige streets, often compared with New York's Fifth Avenue, it was one of the first of the outlying developments to capitalize on the popularity of the automobile. Launched in the 1920's with the opening of the "Miracle Mile", it weathered the Depression, and began accumulating high-class shops, department stores, and business firms. Spaced out along its length are: 37 banks and savings and loan offices, 10 hotels, 17 department stores, 6 churches, 58 office buildings, and countless apartments. With land values on the rise, the Wilshire skyline is also rising — and to ever-increasing heights.

CENTURY CITY—pacesetter for urban renaissance

CURVILINEAR CENTURY PLAZA Hotel rises 20 stories above a recessed mall in the mammoth Century City development in western Los Angeles off Santa Monica Boulevard. The hotel is only two rooms wide — so every guest room has an outside balcony — and is curved to eliminate the "bowling alley look" from the long hallways. A project of Alcoa, all buildings in the complex are generously laden with aluminum building materials. Century City replaces a movie studio (1961) which in turn displaced a ranch (1935) which was part of a Spanish grant.

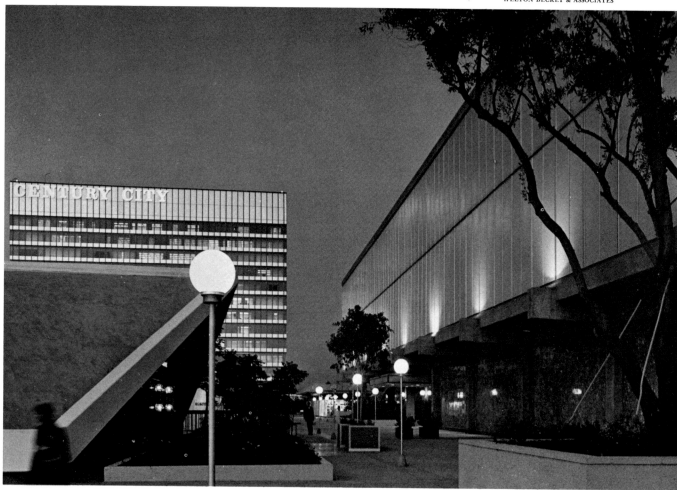

TREES IN SHALLOW PLANT BOXES (including live citrus hung with plastic oranges), decorative and amusing details grace the elevated shopping mall that encircles a major department store in Century City. All parking is underground, walks and roads are scaled for pedestrian use and, in time, a rapid transit terminus will provide swift access to everywhere. Financed wholly by private capital, the $500-million venture will take 15 years to complete, and when finished will have 40 buildings, half of them residential and half commercial, fitted into a 180-acre master plan.

PAUL C. JOHNSON

FRANK GORE

LONG SHADOW OF THE FIRST building in the ambitious Bunker Hill development falls across empty land in the 136-acre site still to be filled with a crop of new buildings (RIGHT). The 40-story Union Bank, one of the first downtown structures to follow the relaxed height limits approved in 1956, occupies only a small portion of its 3.8 acre landscaped site, contains its own parking — six floors of it. Bunker Hill was at one time the Olympus from which the wealthy looked down on the booming city below, but in time, the affluent residents moved elsewhere and their abandoned mansions greatly deteriorated. Approval to clear the land was passed by the city council in 1959 and all buildings (save one) bulldozed to splinters by 1966.

URBAN RENEWAL, the airy shape of the future

THE LOOK OF THE FUTURE, hopefully, is revealed in scale model of the projected Bunker Hill development (buildings completed or under construction in 1968 are tinted in photo), planned to invigorate downtown Los Angeles. Key features: tower apartments for 8,000 residents; combination buildings, half residential, half commercial that will permit people to live in the same building as their work; office buildings for 50,000 people; and internal parking for 20,000 vehicles. Buildings will be widely spaced in a parklike setting, threaded by separated streets and sidewalks that keep pedestrians and vehicles asunder. Requiring astronomical sums for completion, the project will be under construction for years to come.

APPENDIX

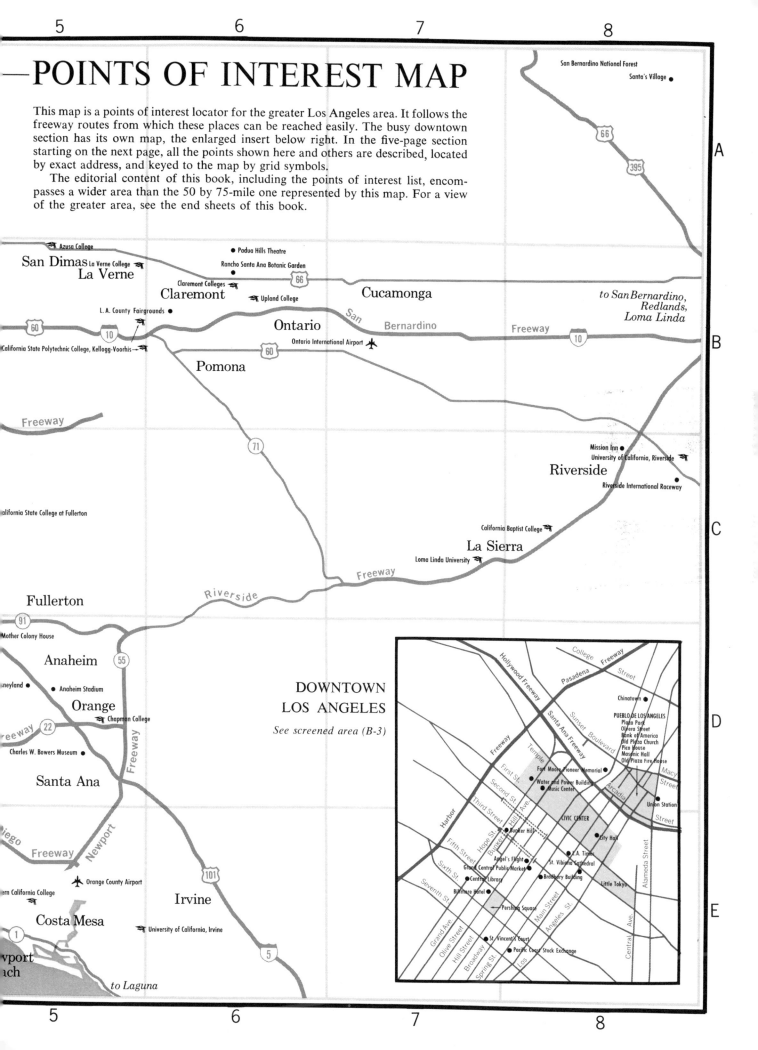

—POINTS OF INTEREST MAP

This map is a points of interest locator for the greater Los Angeles area. It follows the freeway routes from which these places can be reached easily. The busy downtown section has its own map, the enlarged insert below right. In the five-page section starting on the next page, all the points shown here and others are described, located by exact address, and keyed to the map by grid symbols.

The editorial content of this book, including the points of interest list, encompasses a wider area than the 50 by 75-mile one represented by this map. For a view of the greater area, see the end sheets of this book.

San Bernardino National Forest
Santa's Village

66
395

Azusa College
San Dimas La Verne College
La Verne
Padua Hills Theatre
Rancho Santa Ana Botanic Garden
Claremont Colleges
Claremont Upland College
66
Cucamonga
to San Bernardino, Redlands, Loma Linda
L.A. County Fairgrounds
60
10
Ontario
San Bernardino Freeway 10
California State Polytechnic College, Kellogg-Voorhis
Ontario International Airport
Pomona
60

71

Mission Inn
University of California, Riverside
Riverside
Riverside International Raceway

California State College at Fullerton

California Baptist College
La Sierra
Loma Linda University

Freeway

Fullerton
91
Riverside Freeway
Mother Colony House
Anaheim
55
Disneyland Anaheim Stadium
Orange
22 Chapman College
Freeway
Charles W. Bowers Museum
Santa Ana
Newport
Diego Freeway
101
Orange County Airport
Irvine
5
Southern California College
Costa Mesa
1
Newport Beach
University of California, Irvine
to Laguna

DOWNTOWN
LOS ANGELES

See screened area (B-3)

Hollywood Freeway
College Freeway
Pasadena Street
Sunset Boulevard
Chinatown
PUEBLO DE LOS ANGELES
Plaza Park
Olvera Street
Bank of America
Old Plaza Church
Pico House
Masonic Hall
Old Plaza Fire House
Freeway
Temple
First St.
Second St.
Santa Ana Freeway
Fort Moore Pioneer Memorial
Water and Power Building
Music Center
Arcadia
Macy Street
Union Station
Harbor
Third Street
CIVIC CENTER
Hope St.
Bunker Hill
City Hall
Fifth Street
Angel's Flight
L.A. Times
St. Vibiana Cathedral
Grand Central Public Market
Sixth St.
Central Library
Bradbury Building
Little Tokyo
Biltmore Hotel
Seventh St.
Alameda Street
Pershing Square
Grand Ave.
Olive Street
Hill Street
Broadway
Spring St.
Main Street
Los Angeles St.
Central Ave.
St. Vincent's Court
Pacific Coast Stock Exchange

POINTS OF INTEREST

The sheer size of the Los Angeles metropolis tends to hide many of its landmarks from visitor and resident alike, and a list of major points of interest changes with the city year by year.

This section points out and provides some information on interesting sites in Los Angeles, old and new, that you may want to visit or just know about. Entries can be located on the points of interest map on pages 290-91 through their grid symbols.

HISTORICAL FEATURES

BANNING HOUSE (D-3) 401 E. M St., Wilmington. Century-old mansion of Gen. Phineas Banning, who founded Wilmington and opened Port's inner harbor. Now a museum.

DRUM BARRACKS (D-3) 1053 Cary Ave., Wilmington. Only surviving building of a Civil War military post.

LOS CERRITOS RANCH HOUSE MUSEUM (D-3) 4600 Virginia Rd., Long Beach. Period furniture and objects.

LOS ENCINOS STATE HISTORICAL MONUMENT (A-1) La Maida and Moorpark streets, Encino. Once headquarters for Franciscan padres, later an important rancho. Indians' spring and historic buildings remain.

MISSION SAN FERNANDO (A-1) 15151 San Fernando Mission Blvd., San Fernando. Founded 1797; California's largest original mission structure. Rose and cactus gardens.

MISSION SAN GABRIEL (B-4) 537 W. Mission Dr., San Gabriel. Founded 1771. Religious and historical treasures as well as early Indian artifacts.

MOTHER COLONY HOUSE (D-5) 414 N. West St., Anaheim. First house of the German colony, Anaheim (1857). Now an historical museum.

OLD MILL (B-3) 1120 Old Mill Rd., San Marino. First gristmill for Mission San Gabriel (early 1800's). Now a museum.

PIO PICO STATE HISTORICAL MONUMENT (C-4) 6003 Pioneer Blvd., Whittier. Home of California's last Mexican governor.

PUEBLO DE LOS ANGELES STATE HISTORICAL MONUMENT (B-3) See *Downtown Los Angeles.*

DOWNTOWN LOS ANGELES *(See map insert, page 291)*

CIVIC CENTER is clustered around Main, Hope, Temple, and First streets. A monumental progression of public buildings from old landmark City Hall west and up the hill to the new landmark Water and Power building, grouped about a landscaped mall.

WATER AND POWER BUILDING 111 N. Hope St. New structure has tour, view of the city from 15th floor.

MUSIC CENTER for the Performing Arts, First and Grand Ave. 7-acre cultural complex includes *Dorothy Chandler Pavilion* for opera and symphony; *Ahmanson Theatre* for legitimate drama and musical productions; *Mark Taper Forum* for intimate drama, musical events.

CITY HALL 200 N. Spring St. Dedicated 1928. Observation walk and municipal art gallery on 27th floor.

LOS ANGELES TIMES Second and Spring streets. Tour including editorial department, composing room, movie.

ST. VIBIANA CATHEDRAL Second and Main streets. 90 year-old church modeled after one in Barcelona.

LITTLE TOKYO bounded by Central, Los Angeles, First, and Second streets. Authentic Japanese shops and restaurants. Celebration of *Nisei Week* in August.

UNION STATION 800 N. Alameda St. Last great train station built in the U. S. (1939), in mission style with colorful patios.

PUEBLO DE LOS ANGELES STATE HISTORICAL MONUMENT bounded by Santa Ana Frwy., N. Spring, Macy, and Alameda streets. The vicinity of Los Angeles' founding by Spanish governor Felipe de Neve in 1781.

PLAZA PARK Kiosk bandstand, animal-shaped shrubbery.

OLVERA STREET Sunset Blvd. to Macy St. "Oldest street in Los Angeles"; a bit of old Mexico with shops and restaurants. *Avila House* on Olvera is L.A.'s oldest house, now restored.

BANK OF AMERICA on the Plaza. Large display of antique weapons; Mexican-style interior.

OLD PLAZA CHURCH N. Main St. at Sunset Blvd. Adobe church is oldest in L.A. (1822). Gold-leaf altar, frescoed ceilings.

PICO HOUSE N. Main St. Early hotel. *Merced Theater* next to it was city's first. Both restored.

MASONIC HALL N. Main St. Restored first meeting house of Los Angeles Masons.

OLD PLAZA FIRE HOUSE Plaza and Los Angeles streets. Restoration, horse-drawn fire-fighting equipment.

CHINATOWN off N. Broadway near College St. Brightly painted Oriental import shops, restaurants, bakeries. *Chinese New Year* celebration in February.

FORT MOORE PIONEER MEMORIAL Hill St. bet. Hollywood Frwy. and Sunset Blvd. Block-long monumental wall sculpture and waterfall where Gen. Fremont established the L.A. garrison after conquest of Pio Pico, 1874.

PERSHING SQUARE bordered by Hill, Olive, Sixth, and Fifth streets. City park is heart of downtown.

BILTMORE HOTEL 515 S. Olive St. 40 year-old landmark, still largest hotel on coast. Ornate lobby with art gallery, shops.

CENTRAL LIBRARY 630 W. Fifth St. Largest public library west of the Mississippi (4 mill. vols.). Mural-decorated rotunda; excellent early California collection.

BUNKER HILL 300 block of Bunker Hill Ave. bet. Grand and Hope St. One or two houses remain as reminders of former opulence. Now a redevelopment area.

ANGEL'S FLIGHT Third and Hill streets. Shortest incorporated railway in existence and L.A.'s last surviving cable car (1901). Still a 5-cent ride.

GRAND CENTRAL PUBLIC MARKET Hill St. to Broadway near Third St. A block-deep bazaar; fresh produce, international foods.

BRADBURY BUILDING 304 S. Broadway. Early-day architectural gem with cast-iron work, open elevator cages.

PACIFIC COAST STOCK EXCHANGE 618 S. Spring St. Activity timed to New York hours. Visitors gallery.

ST. VINCENT'S COURT between Broadway and Hill on Seventh St. Bookstalls, espresso bar, sidewalk florist.

MUSEUMS

History and Science

CHARLES W. BOWERS MEMORIAL MUSEUM (D-5) 2002 N. Main St., Santa Ana. Exhibits of history and other items in a pleasant little museum.

LOS ANGELES COUNTY MUSEUM OF NATURAL HISTORY (B-3) *Exposition Pk.,* 900 Exposition Blvd. Extensive exhibits emphasizing California history and natural environment including assembled skeletons from La Brea Tar Pits. African and North American animal habitats and relics of prehistoric man.

SOUTHWEST MUSEUM (B-3) 234 Museum Dr., Highland Park. Recreation of Western Indian civilization with exhibits of handicrafts and historical relics. Nearby is the founder's home, *El Alisal,* or *Lummis Home,* 200 E. Ave. 43. Also an early adobe in reproduction, *Casa de Adobe,* 4603 N. Figueroa St.

CALIFORNIA MUSEUM OF SCIENCE AND INDUSTRY (B-3) *Exposition Pk.,* 700 State Dr. Mechanized, do-it-yourself exhibits of natural and industrial resources of the state. Also, special programs, model railroad, Shirley Temple doll collection.

GRIFFITH OBSERVATORY (B-2) *Griffith Pk.,* Vermont Ave. entrance. Telescope and Hall of Science. Planetarium shows reproduce the skies of anytime, any place, include a trip to the moon.

MT. WILSON OBSERVATORY (A-4) 26 mi. no. of Pasadena via Angeles Crest Hwy. Third largest telescope in the world (100-in.), astronomical museum, glassed-in observation gallery atop mile-high peak.

LA BREA TAR PITS (B-2) *Hancock Pk.,* 5801 Wilshire Blvd. Park landscaped to recreate scenes of Glacial Ages when the black pools were death traps for unwary animals. Discovered 1769, pits yielded world's finest Pleistocene fossils. Observation pit building.

FERNDELL NATURE MUSEUM (B-2) *Griffith Pk.,* Red Oak and Ferndell Dr. Plant and animal exhibits, geology of park.

Fine Arts

J. PAUL GETTY MUSEUM (B-1) 17895 W. Pacific Coast Hwy., Malibu. Getty's ranch house, now an art museum. Greek and Roman statuary, Louis XV and XVI furniture, tapestries, paintings by Italian and Dutch masters. By appointment.

HENRY E. HUNTINGTON ART GALLERY AND LIBRARY (B-4) 1151 Oxford St., San Marino. The railroad magnate's original collection in his home. 18th and 19th-century British paintings feature *Blue Boy* and *Pinkie.* Rare tapestries, porcelains, sculpture, and signed period furniture. Rare books and manuscripts in Library including a Gutenberg Bible. (See *Gardens*)

LOS ANGELES COUNTY MUSEUM OF ART (B-2) *Hancock Pk.,* 5905 Wilshire Blvd. Three pavilions comprise largest art museum in the West: *Ahmanson Gallery,* permanent collection; *Special Exhibitions Gallery; Leo S. Bing Center,* theater, art rental, children's gallery. Also *Simon Sculpture Garden.*

LYTTON CENTER OF THE VISUAL ARTS (B-2) 8150 Sunset Blvd. Selections of California artists. Owns large collection of historical objects from the movie industry.

MUNICIPAL ART GALLERIES (B-2) *Barnsdall Pk.,* 4800 Hollywood Blvd. Changing exhibits of many art forms. Adjoining is Frank Lloyd Wright's *Hollyhock House.*

PASADENA ART MUSEUM (A-3) 46 N. Los Robles Ave., Pasadena. Permanent collection strong in German Expressionism, graphic arts. Changing exhibits emphasize contemporary art.

PARKS

BROOKSIDE PARK (A-3) Chevy Chase and Linda Vista Dr., Pasadena. 520 acres of recreational facilities beside the Rose Bowl, includes baseball diamonds, bridle paths, picnic grounds.

BUSCH GARDENS (A-1) 15800 Roscoe Blvd. Brilliantly colored flowers, lakes, lagoons, refreshment pavilions, islands, cliffs, waterfalls, and tropical fowl. Tour including brewery begins on elevated monorail, continues on a boat.

CHATSWORTH PARK (A-1) no. on St. Hwy. 118, west on Chatsworth St. Picnic areas, playground, climbing on rocky Simi Hills. TV and movie westerns shot here.

ECHO PARK (B-3) Glendale Blvd. at Bellevue. Island in a peaceful lake contrasts with the nearby busy city. One of the finest collections of native Southern California palm trees.

EXPOSITION PARK (B-3) 3915 So. Figueroa St. Large culture and sports complex with gardens, contains: *Sports Arena, Memorial Coliseum, Swim Stadium, County Museum of Natural History, California Museum of Science and Industry.*

FOREST LAWN MEMORIAL PARK (B-3) 1712 Glendale Ave., Glendale. Features works of art including replicas of Michelangelo's works and famed "Last Supper" stained glass window.

GRIFFITH PARK (B-2, 3) Los Feliz Blvd. at Riverside Dr. Largest city park in the U. S.; 4,000 acres, mostly hilly wilderness. Complete recreation facilities and attractions listed below.

Los Angeles Zoo is new and groups animals, birds, and plants according to continents to approximate their natural environment. Children can pet and feed small animals at Children's Zoo. Also Greek Theatre; Observatory; Travel Town with the West's best collection of old trains; and Ferndell Nature Museum.

HANCOCK PARK (B-2) 5801 Wilshire Blvd. *L.A. County Museum of Art* and *La Brea Tar Pits* with life-size figures of prehistoric animals.

WILLIAM S. HART RANCH (off map, see A-1) 24151 Newhall Ave., Newhall. Mementos of the cowboy star's movie career, notable Remington and Russell western paintings, range animals, bunkhouse and barn.

JAPANESE DEER PARK (C-4) Santa Ana Frwy. at Knott Ave., Buena Park. Tranquil grounds inspired by the park in Nara, Japan with Dove Pavilion, lagoon, classic Tea House, other animals. Visitors can pet and feed tame deer.

MACARTHUR PARK (B-3) 655 Alvarado St. Named for famed WWII general, subtropical landscape. Lake with boats. Summer programs of Shakespeare, music.

WILL ROGERS STATE HISTORIC PARK (B-1) 14235 Sunset Blvd., Pacific Palisades. Ranch home of the western humorist with tour of house, stables. Polo field and hiking trails.

Gardens and Arboreta

DESCANSO GARDENS (A-3) 1418 Descanso Dr., La Canada. Botanic display blooming year-around, noted for rose, camellia, and native plant gardens. Bird sanctuary, educational displays, and Japanese Tea Pavilion.

ELYSIAN PARK (B-3) Upper Chavez Ravine, enter from N. Broadway. First arboretum in Southern California, many rare specimens. Hiking trails. *All City Outdoor Art Festival* in summer.

HUNTINGTON BOTANICAL GARDENS (B-4) 1151 Oxford Rd., San Marino. 30,000 specimens of trees and shrubs on 280 acres with camellia, azalea, rose gardens, palm and cactus collections; Japanese garden. (See *Museums, Fine Arts*)

LOS ANGELES STATE AND COUNTY ARBORETUM (A-4) 301 N. Baldwin Ave., Arcadia. Thousands of exotic plants, *Sunset's* Demonstration Home Gardens, and jungle where Tarzan movies were made. Also adobe village and "Lucky" Baldwin's historical *Queen Anne Cottage*. Jeep train tour.

RANCHO SANTA ANA BOTANIC GARDEN (B-6) 1500 N. College Ave., Claremont. Many varieties of California native plants. Rock, dune and desert gardens.

ROSE HILLS MEMORIAL PARK (B-4) 3900 Workman Mill Rd., Whittier. *Pageant of Roses and Botanical Gardens*. Hundreds of varieties of roses, including green and purple ones, rare 6-foot Weeping Tree Roses.

SOUTH COAST BOTANICAL GARDEN (D-2) Rolling Hills Rd., near Crenshaw Blvd., Palos Verdes Peninsula. Test and educational garden uniquely established on fill. Plants from many countries.

UCLA BOTANICAL GARDENS (B-1) enter on LeConte or Hilgard Ave., Westwood. Rare shrubs and trees from all over the world. Japanese Garden.

AMUSEMENT PARKS

DISNEYLAND (D-5) 1313 Harbor Blvd., Anaheim. Walt Disney's magic kingdom, divided into four make-believe "lands" for adults as well as children. Open at night with entertainment plus regular raft of rides, bands, hootenannies.

KNOTT'S BERRY FARM (D-4) State Hwy. 39, Buena Park. Complex of shops and restaurants noted for fried chicken and berry pies. Authentic ghost town, and 1849 gold rush community with shows.

NU-PIKE AMUSEMENT PARK (D-3) 55 S. Chestnut Place, Long Beach. Attractions extend for a mile on ocean front.

PACIFIC OCEAN PARK (C-1) 3020 The Promenade, ½ mi. so. of Santa Monica Pier. Seaside amusement park featuring underwater Neptune's Kingdom, Sea Circus, a diving bell, Ocean Skyway.

SANTA'S VILLAGE (A-8) St. Hwy. 18, Lake Arrowhead. Land of make-believe with Santa, Mrs. Claus and active elves. Shops, sleigh ride past gingerbread house and lollipop trees, and puppet theater.

SPORTS ARENAS

ANAHEIM STADIUM (D-5) 2000 State College, Anaheim. Home of the California Angels. Seats 43,402, has 230-ft. scoreboard.

DODGER STADIUM (B-3) Chavez Ravine. Home of the Los Angeles Dodgers. Four-tiered stadium seating 56,000.

LOS ANGELES MEMORIAL COLISEUM (B-3) *Exposition Pk.*, 3911 Figueroa. One of world's largest outdoor stadiums and site of 1932 Olympics. Seats 95,000 for Los Angeles Rams, U.S.C., U.C.L.A. football games; track and field events.

SPORTS ARENA (B-3) *Exposition Pk.*, 3939 S. Figueroa. Indoor arena for trade shows and sports events. Houses L.A. Blades hockey and USC basketball games.

FORUM (C-2) Manchester and Prairie Ave., Inglewood. New home of Lakers basketball and Kings hockey teams.

PAULEY PAVILION (B-1) *UCLA*, Westwood. The Bruins basketball team plays here.

ROSE BOWL (A-3) Arroyo Seco Canyon, Pasadena. Site of the famed New Year's football game, seats 100,000.

HOLLYWOOD PARK (C-2) Century Blvd. and Prairie Ave., Inglewood. Beautifully landscaped for thoroughbred and harness racing. Opportunities to watch morning workouts.

SANTA ANITA PARK (A-4) 285 W. Huntington Dr., Arcadia. Winter thoroughbred racing track, also known for flower-filled infield and view of San Gabriel mountains.

RIVERSIDE INTERNATIONAL RACEWAY (C-8) 22255 Eucalyptus, Riverside. One of nation's top tracks. Major races including *L.A. Times Grand Prix* and *Riverside 500*. Tires and new automotive equipment tested here.

ENTERTAINMENT WORLD

CAPITOL TOWER (B-2) Hollywood and Vine St., Hollywood. First circular office building in the world appropriately housing a record company. Tour.

GRAUMAN'S CHINESE THEATER (B-2) 6925 Hollywood Blvd., Hollywood. World-famous movie theater resembling an enormous Chinese pagoda. Hand and footprints of stars embedded in cement in the courtyard.

CBS TELEVISION CITY (B-2) 7800 Beverly Blvd. Tours of studios, program sets, equipment and wardrobe departments.

NBC COLOR CITY (A-2) 3000 W. Alameda Ave., Burbank. Tours behind-the-scenes at a television studio.

METRO-GOLDWYN-MAYER STUDIO (B-2) 10136 Washington Blvd., Culver City. Tour through cutting rooms, sets, actual shooting of a television series.

UNIVERSAL CITY STUDIOS (A-2) 3900 Lankershim Blvd., Universal City. Tour of sound stages, back lot with exteriors from around the world, star's dressing room. See makeup demonstrations, special effects sets, shows by stunt men.

UNIVERSITIES AND FOUR YEAR COLLEGES

AZUSA COLLEGE (B-5) Hwy. 66 at Citrus Ave., Azusa.

BIOLA COLLEGE (C-4) 13800 Biola Ave., La Mirada.

CALIFORNIA BAPTIST COLLEGE (C-8) 8432 Magnolia Ave., Riverside.

CALIFORNIA INSTITUTE OF THE ARTS (off map, see A-1) Placerita Canyon near Newhall. Merger of L.A. Conservatory of Music and Chouinard Art School. New campus on site of Golden Oak Ranch is corner of a planned city, Valencia.

CALIFORNIA INSTITUTE OF TECHNOLOGY (A-4) 1201 E. California, Pasadena. One of nation's finest technical schools and center for scientific research, founded 1891, for men. Operates NASA's Jet Propulsion Laboratory.

CALIFORNIA LUTHERAN COLLEGE (off map, see A-1) Thousand Oaks.

CALIFORNIA STATE COLLEGE AT DOMINGUEZ HILLS (D-3) 809 E. Victoria St., Gardena.

CALIFORNIA STATE COLLEGE AT FULLERTON (C-5) 800 North State College Blvd., Fullerton. Largest college-oriented community in America. Bookstore is Orange County's largest.

CALIFORNIA STATE COLLEGE AT LONG BEACH (D-4) 6101 E. Seventh St., Long Beach. Outstanding outdoor abstract sculptures left by the International Sculpture Symposium in 1965.

CALIFORNIA STATE COLLEGE AT LOS ANGELES (B-3) 5151 State College Dr. One of nation's major urban centers of higher education; campus has contemporary character.

CALIFORNIA STATE COLLEGE AT SAN BERNARDINO (off map, see B-8) 5500 State College Pkwy., San Bernardino.

CALIFORNIA STATE POLYTECHNIC COLLEGE, KELLOGG-VOORHIS (B-5) Hwy. 99, Pomona; Valley Center near Cyprus Ave., San Dimas. Operates Arabian Horse Farm with shows for the public.

CHAPMAN COLLEGE (D-5) Orange. Founded 1861.

CLAREMONT COLLEGES (B-6) 747 N. Dartmouth, Claremont. Modeled on Oxford plan, distinguished independent schools share selected facilities and *Claremont Graduate School.*

CLAREMONT MEN'S COLLEGE Founded 1947, enrolls some 600 students.

HARVEY MUDD COLLEGE Coed school of about 300 students, emphasizes science and engineering.

PITZER COLLEGE Women's college stressing social sciences.

POMONA COLLEGE The first Claremont school, incorporated 1887, is one of the most selective schools in the country. Has famed Orozco, Lebrun murals.

SCRIPPS COLLEGE Second of the Claremont group, 1926, filled the need for an all-woman college. Art gallery, garden.

IMMACULATE HEART COLLEGE (B-2) 2021 N. Western, Hollywood. Oldest Catholic college for women in Southern California, 1916.

LA VERNE COLLEGE (B-5) 1950 Third Ave., La Verne. Founded 1891.

LOMA LINDA UNIVERSITY Loma Linda (off map, see B-8) and La Sierra (C-7) campuses. Emphasizes healing arts.

LOS ANGELES BAPTIST COLLEGE (off map, see A-1) 21726 West Placerita Canyon Rd., Newhall.

LOS ANGELES PACIFIC COLLEGE (B-3) 625 Coleman Ave.

LOYOLA UNIVERSITY (C-2) 7101 W. 80th St., Westchester. Catholic men's school, founded 1915.

MARYMOUNT COLLEGE (D-2) 6717 Palos Verdes Dr., Palos Verdes Estates. Catholic women's college.

MOUNT ST. MARY'S COLLEGE (B-1) 12001 Chalon Rd., and 10 Chester Place. Independent liberal arts college.

NORTHROP INSTITUTE OF TECHNOLOGY (C-2) 1155 West Arbor Vitae St., Inglewood. College of engineering.

OCCIDENTAL COLLEGE (B-3) 1600 Campus Rd., Eagle Rock. Highly selective. Noted schools of diplomacy, world affairs.

PACIFIC CHRISTIAN COLLEGE (D-3) 4835 E. Anaheim St., Long Beach.

PASADENA COLLEGE (A-4) 1539 E. Howard St., Pasadena.

PEPPERDINE COLLEGE (C-2) 8035 S. Vermont. Palm-covered campus in center of the city. Student-teacher ratio of 13-1.

SAN FERNANDO VALLEY STATE COLLEGE (A-1) 18111 Nordhoff St., Northridge.

SOUTHERN CALIFORNIA COLLEGE (E-5) 2525 Newport Blvd., Costa Mesa. Orange County's oldest four-year school.

UNIVERSITY OF CALIFORNIA, IRVINE (E-5) Irvine. Completed 1965 on 1,000 acre site.

UNIVERSITY OF CALIFORNIA, LOS ANGELES (B-1) 405 Hilgard Ave., Westwood. Outstanding school with 29,000 students. Botanical gardens, ethnic and Dickson art museums.

UNIVERSITY OF CALIFORNIA, RIVERSIDE (C-8) 4045 Canyon Crest Dr., Riverside.

UNIVERSITY OF REDLANDS (off map, see B-8) Redlands.

UNIVERSITY OF SOUTHERN CALIFORNIA (B-2) 3551 University Ave. Largest private university in Southern California, founded 1880. Fisher Art Gallery.

UPLAND COLLEGE (B-6) 792 West Arrow Hwy., Upland.

WHITTIER COLLEGE (C-4) 505 E. Philadelphia, Whittier. Founded by Quakers, 1901. Second largest private school of higher learning in Southern California.

WOODBURY COLLEGE (B-3) 1027 Wilshire Blvd. Noted business school.

MORE POINTS OF INTEREST

FARMER'S MARKET (B-2) Third St. at Fairfax Ave. Open-air stalls, shops, and restaurants, offering array of fresh fruits and vegetables, meats, fish, bakery goods. International gourmet and gift items.

HOLLYWOOD BOWL (B-2) 2301 N. Highland Ave. Large natural amphitheater, holds summer "Symphonies Under the Stars."

LA CIENEGA ART ROW (B-2) 500-900 block. Monday night customary "art walk." Gallery row for art lovers.

LOS ANGELES COUNTY FAIRGROUNDS (B-6) White Ave., Pomona. The site of the "Biggest and Most Beautiful County Fair in America" in September. The landscaped grounds, encircled by a monorail, are used for many shows and exhibitions. Has a steam locomotive collection.

MISSION INN (C-8) Orange St., Riverside. Castlelike inn mixes mission, European, Oriental architectures. Historical doll collection, catacombs, Shrine of Aviators, chapel and Mexican shrine made in 1700's.

MORMON TEMPLE (B-2) 10741 Santa Monica Blvd. Largest of the Mormon temples, a monumental white structure with gold-leaf statue of Angel Moroni on top visible 25 mi. out to sea. Beautiful grounds, movies of interior at Visitors Center.

MOVIELAND WAX MUSEUM (C-4) 7711 Beach Blvd., Buena Park. Likenesses of film stars in their most memorable roles. Tableaux of artists at work on their masterpieces in the *Palace of Living Art.*

PADUA HILLS THEATRE (B-6) Claremont. Plays and pageants in Spanish and English by Mexican players keep alive romantic Spanish and Mexican traditions of California. Also restaurant with entertainment, import shops.

SAN ANTONIO WINERY (B-3) 737 Lamar St. Last producing winery in Los Angeles.

SAINT SOPHIA CATHEDRAL (C-2) 1324 S. Normandie. Greek Orthodox. Stained glass depicting apostles, a profusion of large murals, and 17 crystal chandeliers. Interior decorated with pure gold.

SELF-REALIZATION FELLOWSHIP—LAKE SHRINE (B-1) 17190 Sunset Blvd., Pacific Palisades. A 10-acre retreat for rest and meditation, with lake.

SUNSET STRIP (B-2) Winding 2-mile strip of Sunset Blvd., unincorporated territory bet. Hollywood and Beverly Hills. Site of lavish homes, nightclubs, restaurants, and theatrical agencies.

WATTS TOWERS (C-3) 1765 E. 107th St., Watts. Simon Rodia's vision expressed in concrete, glass, steel, and rubble — folk art fantasy that is truly unique.

WAYFARERS' CHAPEL (D-2) Palos Verdes Dr. S., Portuguese Bend. Unique "Glass Church" and beautiful grounds overlooking the ocean. Designed by Lloyd Wright, dedicated to theologian-mystic Emmanuel Swedenborg.

Major Airports

LOS ANGELES INTERNATIONAL AIRPORT (C-2) One of the most modern jet-age terminals in the country, capable of handling 3 million passengers a year. Major aircraft manufacturing.

LOCKHEED-BURBANK AIRPORT (A-2) Air passenger traffic as well as major aircraft manufacturing.

ONTARIO AIRPORT (B-7) Mostly short-flight traffic. Jet back-up for L.A. International.

ORANGE COUNTY AIRPORT (E-5) Closest service to such Orange County attractions as Disneyland. *Movieland of the Air Museum* located here.

VAN NUYS AIRPORT (A-1) World's busiest corporate aircraft field. No scheduled airlines.

MOUNTAIN WORLD

ANGELES NATIONAL FOREST (A-3) no. and northeast of Los Angeles. Here in the canyons of the San Gabriel Mountains are numerous camping, picnic, and recreation areas mostly located off Angeles Crest Hwy. Six ski areas attract winter sports fans: Mt. Waterman, Kratka Ridge, Table Mt., Blue Ridge, Holiday Hill, Mt. Baldy.

SAN BERNARDINO NATIONAL FOREST (A-8) *Rim-of-the-World Hwy.* is 100-mile scenic loop going through the heart of the mountains, reached by Waterman Canyon, City Creek, or Mill Creek Canyon roads. The two big recreational and residential areas, *Lake Arrowhead* and *Big Bear Lake,* include public camping grounds. The *Palm Springs Tramway* is 2½ mile-long aerial tramway connecting sun and snow sports on Mt. San Jacinto. Ski areas in the San Bernardino Mountains are: Green Valley, Snow Valley, Snow Forest, Snow Summit, Moonridge, and Rebel Ridge.

WATERWORLD

PALISADES CLIFFSIDE PARK (B-1) Palm-landscaped park stretching for 2 mi. along the cliff with view of coastline from Malibu to Palos Verdes Peninsula. Has 1890 camera obscura.

SANTA MONICA PIER AND YACHT HARBOR (B-1) Seafood restaurants and boat and fishing tackle rooms extending 1,680 feet out to sea.

PACIFIC OCEAN PARK (C-1) 3020 The Promenade. (See *Amusement Parks*)

MARINA DEL REY (C-2) 44 Del Rey at Mindanao Way, Venice. The biggest pleasure boat harbor on the Pacific Coast with capacity for 9,000 vessels. 5,000 apartment units on the waterside.

FISHERMAN'S WHARF AND PROMENADE (D-2) Coral Way and Harbor Dr., Redondo Beach. Features seafood restaurants, fish markets, pier fishing.

MARINELAND OF THE PACIFIC (D-2) Palos Verdes Dr. S., Palos Verdes Peninsula. World's largest oceanarium featuring three-ring circus with trained whales, porpoises, sea lions. Thousands of ocean animals and fish. 314-ft. Sky Tower, coastal cruises.

PORT OF LOS ANGELES (D-3) Mammoth man-made harbor began construction in 1899, comprises San Pedro, Wilmington, part of Terminal Island.

CABRILLO BEACH MARINE MUSEUM (E-3) 3720 Stephen White Dr., San Pedro. Displays of shells, marine specimens, ship models, navigation instruments.

FORT MACARTHUR (E-3) Western Ave., San Pedro. Named for Gen. Arthur MacArthur, father of Douglas. Once helped protect the harbor, now headquarters for 47th Artillery Brigade.

PORTS OF CALL VILLAGE (D-3) Berths 76 and 77, Harbor Blvd., San Pedro. Quaint shops, cobblestone streets like early California seaport village. Specialty restaurants and shops representing foreign countries.

WHALER'S WHARF (D-3) Next door to *Ports of Call.* Recalls a 19th-century New Bedford fishing community with restaurants, shops, fish markets, and a ship's chandlery.

FISH HARBOR (D-3) Terminal Island. Fishing boats from many countries unload cargoes into canneries here. Home of world's largest tuna fleet. Streets named after fish.

TERMINAL ISLAND (D-3) Location of major fish canneries, ship building, industrial sites, naval station. Serves both harbors; linked to San Pedro by the Vincent Thomas Bridge, to Long Beach by the new Gerald Desmond Bridge.

LONG BEACH HARBOR (D-3) Important as an international deep water port, industrial center, and resort area, with a 7-mile-long white beach for which it was named.

U. S. NAVAL STATION and Long Beach Naval Shipyard (D-3) Home of the U. S. Pacific Fleet.

PIERPOINT LANDING (D-3) Restaurants, shops, and fishing and cruising activities.

NU-PIKE AMUSEMENT PARK (D-3) 55 So. Chestnut Place. (See *Amusement Parks*)

LONG BEACH ARENA AND AUDITORIUM (D-3) Italian Renaissance bldg. on Rainbow Pier. Large convention center and site of *International Beauty Pageant.*

MARINE STADIUM (D-4) Colorado St., Long Beach. Site of 1932 Olympic marine events, now used for college crew regattas, motorboat races, and water skiing.

LAGUNA BEACH ART COLONY (off map, see E-5) Many cliffside studios, art gallery where artists mingle with guests at tea.

SANTA CATALINA ISLAND (off map, see E-3) 22 mi. offshore, reached by steamer, cruiser, or amphibious airplane. Excepting the town of Avalon, the 21-mile-long island is mountainous wilderness and calm coves that attract fishermen, hikers, riders, golfers, and skin divers. Two bison herds, other animals roam the island.

AVALON One square mile of activity on the eastern shore. Quaint town of waterfront shops introduced by landmark, the formidable Casino building.

UNDERSEA GARDENS (California State Marine Preserve) Abalone Pt., Avalon Bay. Colorful fish and shellfish, deep seaweed forests in this protected area are seen through glass-bottom boats.

ORIGIN OF
PLACE NAMES

ALHAMBRA (LA)—Laid out in 1874 and named for the famous Moorish fortress built above Granada, Spain, which was popularized by Washington Irving's *The Alhambra*.

ANAHEIM (ORANGE) — Literally "home on the Ana" — that is, on the Santa Ana River where in the late 1850's a German colony from San Francisco started a vineyardists' community.

AZUSA (LA) — Derived from the Shoshonean Indian village of *Asuksa-gna* located on a knoll north of the present city. Dr. A. L. Kroeber defines its meaning as "perhaps skunk place," while Dr. John P. Harrington's informant avers that the root *Asuk* means "grandmother."

BEVERLY HILLS (LA) — Named by founder Burton E. Green in 1906-7 after Beverly Farms, Massachusetts — "a pretty name" — where he read in the newspapers that President Taft was vacationing.

BURBANK (LA) — Named in 1887 for Dr. David Burbank, former owner of its acreage, sheepraiser, dentist, and builder of the Burbank Theater in Los Angeles.

CALABASAS (LA) — Derived from "Cañada de las Calabasas" (Spanish), canyon of wild gourds or squashes.

CANOGA PARK (LA) — From name applied in the 1890's by Southern Pacific to its station there — originating, probably, in New York State's town of "Canoga," itself an Indian name.

COACHELLA (Riverside) — A corruption, apparently, of a Spanish word meaning "little shells," because of the shells that cover the valley floor, surviving from old Lake Cahuilla.

CUCAMONGA (San Bernardino) — From a Shoshonean Indian village traditionally meaning "sandy place."

EAGLE ROCK (LA) — A landmark named for its resemblance to an eagle with outspread wings.

EL MONTE (LA) — Meaning "the wooded place" (Spanish), referring to thick willow growth along San Gabriel River.

ELSINORE (Riverside) — "Adopted not from the small city so named in Denmark but rather from the immortality given it by Shakespeare . . . and because it has a pleasant sound" — quoting from the promotional pamphlet (1884) issued by founders William Collier, Donald M. Graham, F. H. Heald.

FIGUEROA STREET (LA) — Bearing a famous Spanish-California name, including that of Governor José Figueroa; of a brother, Francisco; and also of Ramón, who built Casa Figueroa in 1846 (according to its one-time curator, Ana Begué de Packman) at what became 3404 S. Figueroa.

HOLLYWOOD (LA) — Originating in an 1887 subdivision of Cahuenga Valley acreage. The wife of the subdivider (Horace H. Wilcox) is credited with the naming — suggested by that of the summer home of a chance acquaintance who lived near Chicago.

LA PUENTE (LA) — From Rancho La Puente, a name perpetuating making of "the bridge" (Spanish) by members of Portolá Party of 1769 when crossing an arroyo in the area.

LOS ANGELES — In 1781, a small group of settlers named their town "El Pueblo de Nuestra Señora La Reina de Los Angeles de Porciúncula" — "Town of Our Lady, Queen of the Angels of Porciúncula." Spanish and Mexican periods shortened it to "El Pueblo," the American to "Los Angeles."

MALIBU (LA) — From Rancho Topanga Malibu Sequit — preserving names of three Indian villages. Ethnologist John P. Harrington says the meaning of "Malibu" is unknown.

PALOS VERDES (LA) — Name of a rancho — site of San Pedro, Palos Verdes Estates, Rolling Hills, etc. — meaning rancho of the "green trees," originating in the Cañada de Palos Verdes, a canyon lying between Sepúlveda and Lomita boulevards, east of Vermont St. and west of Figueroa St.

PASADENA (LA) — A name coined from the Chippewa Indian language and meaning, possibly, "valley between hills."

PICO BOULEVARD (LA) — Honoring Pío Pico, last governor of Mexican California, and his brother Andrés Pico who commanded the California forces at the Battle of San Pascual.

REDONDO BEACH (LA) — From Rancho Sausal Redondo, meaning ranch of the "round clump of willows" (Spanish).

RODEO DE LAS AGUAS (LA) — A rancho, site of Beverly Hills, meaning "the gathering of the waters" (Spanish) and derived from the meeting of streams that in rainy months rushed down Cold Water and Benedict canyons creating a chain of lakes and swamps in the lower lands.

SAN MARINO (LA) — With probable origin in the name of the tiny European republic, but coming to Southern California via a Maryland plantation (birthplace of J. de Barth Shorb) and of the later Shorb estate in San Gabriel Valley — a name retained by purchaser Henry E. Huntington.

SANTA MONICA (LA) — Derived directly from the rancho on which it was laid out — San Vicente y Santa Monica — and indirectly from the stream flowing through the Santa Monica canyon.

SEPULVEDA BOULEVARD (LA) — A street which follows, in part, the northeast boundary of Rancho San Vicente y Santa Monica, once owned by Francisco Sepúlveda.

SIMI (Ventura) — Rancho and town derived from the name of a Chumash Indian village.

SPRING STREET (LA) — Named by Lieutenant E. O. C. Ord (who was the surveyor of Los Angeles City Map No. 1 in 1849) in honor of his Santa Barbara sweetheart, Trinidad Ortega, whom he called his "Springtime" — Primavera. On the map the street was given its Spanish name of "Calle Primavera" and its English equivalent of "Spring Street."

TARZANA (LA) — Former home of Edgar Rice Burroughs, creator of the "Tarzan" stories, whose neighbors voted to called their community "Tarzana."

TUJUNGA (LA) — Derived directly from the rancho of that name and ultimately from an Indian village, so called, with the possible meaning of "mountain range."

WATTS (LA) — From the name (Julia A. Watts) of one of the subdividers of a part of Rancho Tajuata originally owned by Anastacio Abila, the first Negro dwellers being employees of the Pacific Electric Railroad Company.

WHITTIER (LA) — One-time Quaker colony named in 1887 for the New England Quaker poet John Greenleaf Whittier.

WILMINGTON (LA) — Named by founder Phineas Banning after his hometown of Wilmington, Delaware.

WILSHIRE BOULEVARD (LA) — Launched 1896 as de luxe, four-blocks-long, residential street by H. Gaylord Wilshire, Socialist, lecturer, editor, publisher, and fantastic promoter.

BY W. W. ROBINSON

297

CHRONOLOGY

1769 White men visit the Los Angeles area for the first time, they being members of a Spanish exploration party led by Gaspar de Portolá.
"It has all the requisites for a large settlement." (Father Crespi, diarist of the party, in an entry made August 2, 1769)

1771 Mission San Gabriel is established — the first white settlement in Los Angeles County.
"Within the stockade is the Church built of poles and roofed with tules; the dwelling of the Fathers with the workshop, etc., and the granary, all constructed of poles and roofed with tules," etc. (Father Francisco Palou's report to the Viceroy on December 10, 1773)

1781 Los Angeles is born on September 4, as a Spanish pueblo, its settlers being 44 men, women, and children who have been recruited and outfitted in Sonora and Sinaloa, Mexico. The heads of families, all farmers, are of Indian, Negro, and Spanish ancestry.
"They founded the town . . . under the name of Our Lady of the Angels of Porciúncula." (Palou, 1787)

1784 The granting of California's ranchos is begun, with three retirement-minded soldiers — Dominguez, Verdugo, and Nieto — from the Presidio of San Diego. They are permitted by the Governor to graze their stock within non-pueblo areas in what is now Los Angeles and Orange counties.
Too young for retirement, Verdugo sends his brother on ahead. By 1797, however, he has "five small girls and one small child" and is weary of Army life. Urgently he writes to the Governor: "I find myself much afflicted with dropsy, as is well known, for which reason, feeling myself entirely incapable for all duty as a sentinel or as a scout, I . . . solicit my retirement." The Governor's reply is "Yes."

1792 The Tar Pits — later to become famous for their prehistoric relics of the Pleistocene period — are visited by a Spanish scientist who observes bones strewn about.
"In hot weather animals have been seen to sink in it (the lake) and when they tried to escape they were unable to do so, because their feet were stuck, and the lake swallowed them. After many years their bones have come up through the holes, as if petrified. I have brought away several specimens." (José Longinos Martinez in "California in 1792")

1793 Captain George Vancouver sails up the Southern California coast on his voyage of discovery.
"A very advantageous settlement is established on a fertile spot somewhere in this neighborhood . . . called Pueblo de Los Angeles, 'the country town of the Angels'." (Vancouver, 1798)

1818 A site is chosen for Los Angeles' present Plaza and

1818 Cont. Church — and, probably, the Avila House is built, the latter still standing in Olvera Street as the city's oldest private residence.
The walls of the Church rose slowly, aided by a building fund started by the townsmen's sale of 500 cattle and of the 7 barrels of brandy given by Mission San Gabriel, supplemented by the contributions of cattle, mules, wine, and brandy from missions farther away and by heavy fines paid by two prominent Angelenos caught smuggling on the beach of Malibu. (Data from Bancroft)

1822 The Spanish regime in Upper California gives way to Mexican, and a council form of city government is fully established in Los Angeles.

1827-8 A French traveler, Auguste Bernard Duhaut-Cilly, visits California and includes a trip to Los Angeles.
"What struck me chiefly on entering this village was the air of cheerfulness, ease and neatness, which, it seemed to me characterized the inhabitants, and which I had not observed at any of the presidios." (From Duhaut-Cilly's own account)

1835 The status of Los Angeles is raised to that of a city (ciudad).

1836 Richard Henry Dana pays a farewell visit to Los Angeles Harbor.
"Two days brought us to San Pedro and two days more (to our no small joy) gave us our last view of that place which was universally called the hell of California . . . Not even the last view could bring out one feeling of regret." (Dana in his "Two Years Before the Mast")

1840 Los Angeles' first eccentric — William Money of Scotland — arrives in town.
"By a singular circumstance I was born with four teeth and the likeness of the rainbow in my right eye." (One of the opening statements in Money's "Reform of the New Testament Church," published in 1854, apparently the first book printed in Los Angeles)

1842 Sir George Simpson (of Hudson's Bay Company) sails the Southern California coast.
"The Pueblo of Nuestra Señora . . . contains a population of five hundred souls, and is the noted abode of the lowest drunkards and gamblers of the country. This den of thieves is situated . . . in one of the loveliest and most fertile districts of California." (From Simpson's narrative of his journey around the world)

1842 (October) On the false rumor that the United States had declared war on Mexico, the American flag is raised over Monterey. Commodore Thomas Ap Catesby Jones of the United States Navy, who does the flag-raising, calls on Governor Micheltorena in Los

1842
Cont. Angeles the following January of 1843 to apologize. The visit turns into a most festive affair.

"A banquet was given . . . winding up with a grand ball . . . All the wealth and beauty of Los Angeles and surrounding country were present. The commodore and his officers expressed themselves as highly delighted. They also spoke flatteringly of Los Angeles and its neighborhood, calling it the Eden of the earth . . . They were delighted with the California wines." (William Heath Davis in his "Seventy-five Years in California")

1845 Los Angeles is made the capital of Upper California.
"The time has arrived when the City of the Angels begins to figure in the political orb . . . Although it is a small city, it should proceed to show its cleanliness, magnificence and brilliancy in such a manner that the traveler who visits us may say: 'I have seen the City of the Angels. I have seen its police and all demonstrated that it is the Mexican paradise'." (From Leonardo Cota's proposition, recommending the repair and whitewashing of house fronts, approved on April 19, 1845 by the City Council)

1846-7 War between the United States and Mexico.

1848 California is ceded to the United States through the Treaty of Guadalupe Hidalgo.

1849 Los Angeles, owner, as a Spanish pueblo, of four square leagues of land, employs Lieutenant E. O. C. Ord of the U. S. Army to survey the heart of its area, so that it might auction off lots to fill an empty treasury.
"Our map is finished and is a very pretty one." (Letter from William Rich Hutton, Ord's assistant, to an uncle, written on September 1, 1849)

1850 Los Angeles is incorporated and the city and county governments are organized under laws passed by the first American legislature.

1852 Horace Bell, destined to write the distinguished and flamboyant "Reminiscences of a Ranger," arrives to become a citizen of Los Angeles.

"We hied us to the classic precincts of the Calle de los Negros, . . . which was the most perfect and full grown pandemonium that this writer . . . has ever beheld." (Bell, describing a first view of the City of the Angels)

1857 The boom, caused by the demand for beef cattle from Gold Rush miners, collapses, with gamblers and outlaws getting out of Los Angeles as fast as they had come in.

1860's The ranchos are broken up, following their owners' suffering of a series of drought years, of heavy debts, of excessively high interest rates, of title problems, of foreclosures, and of squatterism. The agricultural era begins, including the commercial planting of orange groves.

1876 The Southern Pacific Railroad comes to Los Angeles, ending the town's isolation and making possible the later waves of immigration.
"The valley of Los Angeles can easily hold a million inhabitants, although it now supports less than 20,000 . . . Los Angeles is destined to become the second most important city in the state." (Ludwig Louis Salvator, a German observer of 1876, whose book was published in Germany in 1878)

1887-8 The real estate boom of the Eighties — most fantastic of all booms — draws an enormous immigration and

1887-8
Cont. establishes much of the present pattern of the communities of the Los Angeles area.
From an advertisement of South Cucamonga Townsite appearing on a typical promotional map of the period: "The distance from the Sea-Coast assures freedom from Fog-laden Sea-breezes, while the atmosphere is so pure, dry and exhilarating, that those suffering from Asthmatic and Pulmonary troubles find it most invigorating and health restoring . . . No new Town in Southern California has brighter prospects for becoming a Railroad Center than South Cucamonga."

1892 Oil is discovered in Los Angeles by E. L. Doheny.

1909 Los Angeles literally faces the blue Pacific, from its own Port of Los Angeles created by a consolidation with San Pedro and Wilmington (following the Shoestring Annexation of 1906 which had given the metropolis a toehold on the ocean).

1910 The first movie is made in Hollywood (in a tavern and barn at the corner of Sunset Boulevard and Gower Street) in the same year in which it is consolidated with Los Angeles.
"The legendary Hollywood is a sort of Venice without canals, full of glittering conveyances, dazzling maidens, and men like gods . . . Marble swimming pools abound . . . and champagne flows everywhere." (Leo C. Rosten in "Hollywood," 1941)

1913 Los Angeles imports its first water — by aqueduct from Owens Valley — to be followed by other importations from Mono Basin, from the Colorado River, and from the Feather River Project.
"There it is, take it!" (Engineer William Mulholland on November 5, 1913)

1941 Los Angeles launches its spectacular freeway system with the dedication of the first one, the Arroyo Seco (or Pasadena) Freeway.
"Helps California drivers get to their accidents sooner." (Bob Hope's crack at the opening of the Hollywood Freeway)

1943 Smog is first noted in Los Angeles — and by 1947 an air pollution control board is empowered "to control everything released into the air in the 4,000 square miles of the Los Angeles Basin."
"Los Angeles . . . awoke the nation to the perils of air pollution." Saturday Evening Post, October 8, 1966)

1953 The development of "El Pueblo de Los Angeles State Historical Monument" is begun — through a master plan and agreement entered into between the state, the city, and the county — to preserve and recreate much of Los Angeles pueblo days centering about the present plaza.

1962 A Cultural Heritage Board is established for the City of Los Angeles through an ordinance passed by the city council and approved by Mayor Sam Yorty. It acts under the jurisdiction of the Municipal Art Department, and its activities have resulted in the preservation of many buildings of historical and architectural significance, as well as of historical sites and noteworthy trees.

1967 Los Angeles, on September 4, 1967, celebrated its 186th birthday, recalling the simplicity of its founding and its development into what *Fortune* magazine has called the "prototype of the supercity."

BY W. W. ROBINSON

299

READING LIST

From an enormous literature about Los Angeles and its environs, I have chosen fourscore books characteristic of the changing city, from the era of Indians and ranchos, the great land and tourist boom of the last century, through depression and wars, to the current explosion of the biggest boom of all.

The vitality of Los Angeles has always excited writers to extreme reactions of love and hate, fascination and disgust, romanticism and satire. Unlike San Francisco, loved by everyone, Los Angeles divides people into either boosters or debunkers, such as Harry Carr and Morrow Mayo, John Chapman and Richard Lillard, to cite four authors whose divergent volumes I have included.

Novels about Los Angeles and Southern California, from romantic *Ramona* (1884) to savage *The Loved One* (1948), illustrate this range of feelings. The gamut is also run in movie novels, from *Merton of the Movies* (1922) to *What Makes Sammy Run* (1941). I have included a generous selection from this field, in the belief that a good work of fiction is a better guide than a bad work of fact.

There is no single bibliography on Los Angeles. Selective lists are to be found in some of the works cited. J. Gregg Layne's *Books of the Los Angeles District* (1950) and my own *Land of Fiction* (1952) are personal choices of nonfiction and novels respectively. W. W. Robinson's *What They Say About the Angels* (1942) is an illuminating harvest of brickbats and bouquets.

Periodicals with abundant material about Los Angeles include Lummis's *Land of Sunshine* (1894-1901), later called *Out West* (1901-1910); the Automobile Club of Southern California's *Touring Topics* (1909-1933), whose title was changed in 1934 to *Westways;* and *Los Angeles Magazine* (1956-   ), especially good on current happenings.

New copies of many of the books I have listed are currently available in bookstores and public libraries, but some are out-of-print as of this writing. The out-of-print books would still be available in most libraries and in some secondhand bookstores. However, readability and fidelity, rather than rarity, have been my criteria of choice.

LAWRENCE CLARK POWELL

THE GOLDEN YEARS

Baur, John E. *The Health Seekers of Southern California, 1870-1900.* San Marino, 1959. And still they come.

Cleland, Robert Glass *The Cattle on a Thousand Hills: Southern California, 1850-1880.* San Marino, 1951. The best of all studies of the rancho era, based on manuscript materials in the Huntington Library.

　—*The Irvine Ranch of Orange County, 1810-1950.* San Marino, 1952. Only today is this greatest of the surviving ranchos being subdivided. This is another of Dr. Cleland's source histories, written with accuracy and style.

Crump, Spencer *Ride the Big Red Cars.* Los Angeles, 1962. Best of all books about the Pacific Electric Railway, Henry E. Huntington's network which bound the suburbs to the city and which was finally made obsolete by the multiplication of the motor car.

Dumke, Glenn S. *The Boom of the Eighties in Southern California.* San Marino, 1944. Excellent study of the great real estate madness, written by today's chancellor of the state colleges, based on source materials in the Huntington Library.

Fink, Augusta *Time and the Terraced Land.* Berkeley, 1966. A charming history of the great headland between Redondo and San Pedro called by the Spaniards "Los Palos Verdes."

The First Los Angeles City and County Directory, 1872, reproduced in facsimile, with an Introduction by Ward Ritchie. Los Angeles, 1963. Contains the first printed listing of the inhabitants, is the first history of the area, and is a colorful typographical riot, the advertisements fully as informative as the text by J. M. Guinn.

Gillingham, Robert C. *The Rancho San Pedro: the Story of a Famous Rancho in L.A. County, of its Owners, the Dominguez Family.* Los Angeles, 1961. Cattle, agriculture, and oil.

Johnston, Bernice Eastman *California's Gabrielino Indians.* Los Angeles, 1962. Authentic study of the aboriginal culture of the Los Angeles area before it was destroyed by the white men, as well as a vivid evocation of a landscape before it was buried under concrete and asphalt.

McPherson, William *Homes in Los Angeles City and County.* Los Angeles, 1883 (1961). A facsimile reproduction of what is said to be the city's first booster publication. Illustrations and advertisements are equally enthralling.

Meadows, Don *Historic Place Names in Orange County.* Balboa Island, 1966. Authentic local history written with perception and style.

Rice, William B. *The Los Angeles Star, 1851-1864: the Beginnings of Journalism in Southern California.* Berkeley and Los Angeles, 1947. From the surviving issues of this rough and ready pioneer newspaper, the author drew rich details of everyday life.

Robinson, W. W., and L. C. Powell *The Malibu.* Los Angeles, 1958. History of and essays about this celebrated rancho which was held inviolate by the Rindge family until in 1928 the state forced a right of way for what became Coast Highway.

Ross, Robert Erskine *Wings Over the Marshes: Shooting Sketches from an Old Log Book.* London, 1948. Nostalgic account of the Los Angeles plain around the turn of the century when the coast was a vast swampy bird refuge.

Salvator, Ludwig Louis *Los Angeles in the Sunny Seventies: A Flower from the Golden Land.* Los Angeles, 1929. Translation by Marguerite Eyer Wilbur of a German traveler's view of what was then a quiet country town.

Smith, Sarah Bixby *Adobe Days.* Los Angeles, 1931. The author's father and uncle drove sheep overland to California. She was born in San Juan Bautista in 1871, then grew up in Los Angeles and on the Rancho Los Cerritos in the Long Beach area. Mrs. Smith's book recaptures the poetry of everyday life in simple, perceptive prose.

Truman, Major Ben C. *Semi-Tropical California*. San Francisco, 1874. Booster literature at its beguiling best by a great beater of the big bass drum.

PIONEERS

Bell, Major Horace *Reminiscences of a Ranger*. Los Angeles, 1881. Reprinted in the 1920's and 1930's and deserving of still another issue, this racy narrative is juicy with the scandal and uproar of frontier life.

Bingham, Edwin *Charles F. Lummis, Editor of the Southwest*. San Marino, 1955. Colorful Yankee who edited the *Los Angeles Times*, founded the monthly *Land of Sunshine*, established the Southwest Museum, led movements to save the redwoods and restore the missions, wrote superbly of the Southwest, and coined the phrase, "See America First."

Block, Eugene B. *Above the Civil War*. Berkeley, 1966. Biography of Thaddeus Lowe, the Balloon Corps pioneer who came to Southern California after the Civil War and built the scenic railway up the mountain back of Pasadena which bears his name.

Dakin, Susanna Bryant *A Scotch Paisano: Hugo Reid's Life in California, 1832-1852*. Berkeley and Los Angeles, 1939. Reid married an Indian woman and pioneered in the area now called San Marino-Pasadena. Another of the superb studies based on Huntington Library sources.

Graves, Jackson A. *My Seventy Years in California*. Los Angeles, 1927. The author is typical of the solid agricultural and mercantile pioneering on which the city's prosperity was based.

Krythe, Maymie *Port Admiral: Phineas Banning, 1830-1885*. San Francisco, 1957. Sympathetic biography of the man whose stubborn vision pioneered the port of Los Angeles known as San Pedro-Wilmington.

Newmark, Harris *Sixty Years in Southern California (1853-1913)*. Boston, 1930. 3rd and best edition of a pioneer merchant's memoirs.

Robinson, W. W. *Lawyers of Los Angeles*. Los Angeles, 1959. Because lawyers are deeply involved in the city's varied life, this superb study is actually a kind of biographical history of Los Angeles, based on source materials, as is everything written by Robinson.

Wolsey, Serge G. *Call House Madame*. San Francisco, 1942. She, too, pioneered as an entrepreneuse in the oldest profession. This naughty memoir is laid in Los Angeles during the teens and twenties and is said to be authentic.

HISTORIES AND CRITIQUES

Carr, Harry *Los Angeles, City of Dreams*. New York, 1935. Long-time columnist of the *Los Angeles Times* writes lyrically of a city destined to be violently altered by the industrialization and immigration which followed World War II.

Chapman, John L *Incredible Los Angeles*. New York, 1967. A comparative newcomer in the role of booster, finds Los Angeles lovable in spite of smog, traffic, fire, drought, and what have you.

Friis, Leo J. *Orange County Through Four Centuries*. Santa Ana, 1965. An excellent local history of the area that has been almost unrecognizably urbanized since World War II.

Gilbert, Richard *City of the Angels*. London, 1964. A young Englishman's account of Los Angeles as it appeared to him while he was in residence at UCLA.

Griffith, Beatrice *American Me*. Boston, 1948. The Mexican-American minority is written about with insight and sympathy.

Hancock, Ralph *Fabulous Boulevard*. New York, 1949. Lively account of Wilshire Boulevard from city to sea.

Layne, J. Gregg *Annals of Los Angeles*. San Francisco, 1935. The city's beginnings as revealed by documents and other source material.

Lillard, Richard G. *Eden in Jeopardy*. New York, 1966. Deeply, widely, solidly researched sociological study by a concerned native Angeleno of the effect of accelerated urbanization and alteration of the natural environment.

McCone Committee *Violence in the City: An End or a Beginning*. Los Angeles, 1965. This report of the Governor's committee, chaired by John A. McCone, on the Watts riots is required reading for an understanding of this deep-rooted minority problem.

McWilliams, Carey *Southern California Country: an Island on the Land*. New York, 1946. Critical, yet affectionate, this study by a local lawyer-journalist was the most searching sociological account of the city yet to be written, and it still remains one of the best.

Mayo, Morrow *Los Angeles*. New York, 1933. First of the debunking narratives, short on historical accuracy, long on lively prejudices, and stringent in its account of the city's "rape" of the Owens River Valley's water resources.

Murphy, Bill *Dolphin Guide to Los Angeles and Southern California*. Garden City, 1962. An excellent paperback, packed with facts, presented without prejudice or any particular point of view.

Nadeau, Remi *Los Angeles from Mission to Modern City*. New York, 1960. Eminently readable, fond, frank, study of the changed and changing city, written by a descendant of a pioneer family.

O'Dell, Scott *Country of the Sun: Southern California, an Informal History and Guide*. New York, 1957. Frankly for tourists, affectionate in tone.

Robinson, W. W. *Los Angeles from the Days of the Pueblo*. San Francisco, 1959. Excellent brief introductory history, sponsored by the California Historical Society.

—*Panorama: A Picture History of Southern California*. Los Angeles, 1953. Best of all books of its kind in choice of unhackneyed pictures and skillful captioning.

—*Ranchos Become Cities*. Pasadena, 1939. As long-time historian of the Title Insurance and Trust Co., the author established himself through works such as this and many pamphlets as the authority on the development of the city's suburbs.

Rolle, Andrew F. *Los Angeles: A Student's Guide to Localized History*. New York, 1965. Occidental College's leading historian here offers young people a useful entry into urban study.

Walker, Franklin *A Literary History of Southern California*. Berkeley and Los Angeles, 1950. An admirable, sympathetic account of all aspects of writing about the region.

Willard, Charles Dwight *History of Los Angeles City*. Los Angeles, 1901. The first serious work of its kind, written by the long-time secretary of the Chamber of Commerce.

Wilson, J. Albert *History of Los Angeles County*. Oakland, 1880. Typical of the series of booster books on California counties, invaluable for contemporary pictorial and biographical material.

Writers' Project *Los Angeles: A Guide to the City and Its Environs.* New York, 1941. Good as far as it went, this WPA work is now indispensable for its evocation of the city that was.

NATURAL HISTORY

Annals of Association of American Geographers *Man, Time, and Space in Southern California.* Chicago, 1956. Enthralling essays by several authorities on the geography and ecology of the Los Angeles area.

Bailey, Harry P. *The Climate of Southern California.* Berkeley and Los Angeles, 1966. One of the University's Natural History paperbacks, explaining such mysterious matters as Temperature Inversion, Prevailing Westerly, Catalina Eddy, and Santa Ana Wind.

Cunningham, Glenn, ed. *Day Tours: Geographical Journeys in the Los Angeles Area.* Palo Alto, 1964. For those whose interest goes beyond Disneyland and Marineland, the movie and TV studios.

Fultz, Francis M. *The Elfin Forest.* Los Angeles, 1923. The classic work on the chaparral, the composite scrub vegetation which mantles the slopes of Southern California's lower mountains and hills and makes all too ideal a fuel for the periodic brush fires.

Jaeger, Edmund C. and Arthur C. Smith *Introduction to the Natural History of Southern California.* Despite proliferating urbanization much of the land still remains natural. Here is an ideal description of it, written by experts, in the University of California's Natural History paperback series.

Nadeau, Remi *The Water Seekers.* New York, 1950. The drama of Los Angeles' unslakeable thirst.

Padilla, Victoria *Southern California Gardens.* Berkeley and Los Angeles, 1961. Beautifully written and illustrated monograph on the pioneers whose love of natural beauty transformed the region into a botanist's paradise.

ARTS AND SCIENCES

Gebhard, David and Robert Winter *A Guide to Architecture in Southern California.* Los Angeles, 1965. Ideal work in conception and execution, handsomely printed in paperback format.

Gordon, Dudley C. *The Cultural Assets of Metropolitan Los Angeles.* Los Angeles, 1940. Museums, galleries, libraries as they flourished between wars.

Moore, Ernest Carroll *I Helped Make a University.* Los Angeles, 1952. The story of UCLA by its first provost.

Politi, Leo C. *Bunker Hill, Los Angeles: Reminiscences of Bygone Days.* Palm Desert, 1964. Paintings and text by one who knew and loved this urban escarpment and its Victorian dwellings whose renewal meant removal.

Robinson, W. W., ed. *A Bookman's View of Los Angeles.* Los Angeles, 1961. Essays by several authorities on the bookish resources of the region.

—*Story of the Southwest Museum.* Los Angeles, 1960. Standing castle-like on the west bank of the Arroyo Seco, between Los Angeles and Pasadena, this museum is devoted entirely to the culture of the American Indian.

Rosten, Leo C. *Hollywood.* New York, 1941. The best of all histories of the moving picture art-business-industry.

Schad, Robert O. *Henry Edwards Huntington, the Founder and the Library.* San Marino, 1948. A pamphlet on the man whose railway wealth established and maintains a great library and museum devoted to Anglo-American culture.

Sunset *Art Treasures in the West.* By the Editors of Sunset. Menlo Park, 1966. Includes museums and galleries of the Los Angeles area.

Woodbury, David O. *The Glass Giant of Palomar.* New York, 1939. One of the world's great telescopes and observatories is located on Palomar Mountain between Los Angeles and San Diego.

Yavno, Max and Lee Shippey *The Los Angeles Book.* Boston, 1950. Yavno's photographs make this a desirable book.

NOVELS

Cain, James M. *The Postman Always Rings Twice.* New York, 1934. Marked by the brutal violence of a shifting, shiftless, Depression-blighted society.

Chandler, Raymond *The Raymond Chandler Omnibus.* New York, 1964. Includes his four masterpieces of detective fiction — *The Big Sleep, The High Window, Farewell My Lovely, The Lady in the Lake* — which marvelously evoke the ambiance of the city in the 1920's and 1930's.

Fenton, Frank *A Place in the Sun.* New York, 1942. Romantic novel of a young crippled immigrant from the Midwest who comes to Los Angeles in search of health and finds heartbreak.

Fitzgerald, F. Scott *The Last Tycoon.* New York, 1941. By the time he came to write this last novel, Fitzgerald had wasted most of his great talent. Still it offers a shrewd appraisal of film-making in Hollywood.

Huxley, Aldous *After Many a Summer Dies the Swan.* New York, 1940. In this novel and the later *Ape and Essence,* the famed English intellectual satirized the foibles of his adopted home-city.

Jackson, Helen Hunt *Ramona.* Boston, 1884. A romantic fictional tract against the injustices suffered by the Indians of Southern California.

Lurie, Alison *The Nowhere City.* New York, 1966. The campus at UCLA, psychiatry, electronics, beatniks of Venice are the stuff of this satirical novel.

Luther, Mark Lee *The Boosters.* Indianapolis, 1923. A shrewd, faithful, affectionate view of the city between wars, a time when real-estate promotion was the greatest madness.

Schulberg, Budd *What Makes Sammy Run.* New York, 1941. The savage anatomy of a Hollywood "heel."

Viertel, Peter *The Canyon.* New York, 1940. Tender story of boyhood, growth, and change in Santa Monica Canyon. A lament for the urbanization of a pastoral backwater, which could be duplicated myriad times as the widening stain of the city has spread over the land.

Waugh, Evelyn *The Loved One.* Boston, 1948. A conservative English Catholic saw a typical Los Angeles memorial park and was moved to this Swiftian satire on local burial customs.

West, Jessamyn *South of the Angels.* New York, 1960. A romantic, large-scale novel of several generations engulfed by the proliferating Queen of the Angels.

West, Nathanael *The Day of the Locust.* New York, 1939. Hollywood hangers-on in the Depression, fueled with alcohol.

Wilson, Harry Leon *Merton of the Movies.* Garden City, 1922. One of the earliest and, even to this day, best of the movie novels, written when cinema was more art than business, packed with vivid details of life on the sets.

INDEX